JOHN HENRY NEWMAN

His Life and Work

BRIAN MARTIN

JOHN HENRY NEWMAN
His Life and Work

NEW YORK
OXFORD UNIVERSITY PRESS
1982

ACKNOWLEDGEMENTS OF ILLUSTRATIONS

Permission to reproduce illustrations is acknowledged as follows: The Birmingham Oratory 1, 2, 4, 5, 15, 18, 21, 22, 24, 26, 27, 28, 32, 33, 34, 35, 36, 37, 39, 40, 43, 44, 45, 47, 48, 50, 51, 52, 53; The London Borough of Ealing Library Service 3; Thomas-Photos, Oxford 6, 12; The Brompton Oratory, London 7, 29, 31, 46; The Provost and Fellows of Oriel College, Oxford 8, 11, 16; The National Portrait Gallery, London 9, 14, 49; Oxford University Press 10; The President and Fellows of Magdalen College, Oxford 13; The Warden and Fellows of Keble College, Oxford 19, 41; The Vicar of St Mary and St Nicholas Church, Littlemore 20; The Bodleian Library, Oxford 23, 42; The National Gallery of Ireland, Dublin 25; The President and Fellows of Trinity College, Oxford 38.

Contents

For Peggy Lou

Preface

JOHN HENRY, CARDINAL NEWMAN (1801–1890) was one of the most brilliant, controversial, far-seeing figures of the nineteenth century. His influence has spread far beyond the country of his birth, the century in which he lived, and the church in which he ended his life: he is not only of great importance in the history of religious thought but is known to a much wider circle for his hymns, his books, the text of Elgar's *The Dream of Gerontius* and the Oratories he founded in Birmingham and London. He is widely loved and remembered – by Catholics and non-Catholics alike – as a saintly and gentle figure: yet his conversion to the Church of Rome sparked off one of the bitterest and most divisive controversies of the Victorian age, and one which lost him friends and respect, and was, for many years, to sever him from his beloved university of Oxford. He is important in the history of Roman Catholicism because many of his ideas disregarded under the pontificate of Pius IX but more favoured under Leo XIII, were, in the end, to be adopted by the second Vatican Council almost a century later in the 1960s.

The publication over recent years of Newman's letters and diaries has enabled a better understanding of him and his achievement than ever existed before. It is largely on the evidence of these, his own writings, that this biography rests. He himself would have greatly approved the meticulous work of C. S. Dessain, Ian Ker and Thomas Gornall, and I have tried not to interpret too much, in Newman's own words, 'Lord Burleigh's nods'. Early biographies of Newman, such as Wilfrid Ward's, and Meriol Trevor's more recent work, have all been invaluable in this particular study; and without the generous co-operation of Gerard Tracey, and the Birmingham Oratory, I should not have got very far in my researches. The Oratory has kindly allowed me to quote at will from the letters and diaries (published by Oxford University Press) for which it holds the copyright: I have kept Newman's original spellings and punctuation. The Warden and Fellows of Keble College, Oxford, have been characteristically, and consistently, kind in allowing me to use the resources of their library, and the President and Fellows of Trinity College have allowed me to make use of their College's breviarium of stories about Thomas Short. I am also indebted to the copyright-holder of Anne Pollen's unpublished diary for allowing me to quote from her writings.

Those who might have come upon this book not knowing anything at all about Newman, will be able to leave it, I hope, enlightened and introduced to the 'cloistral, silver-veined prose of Newman' which James Joyce admired. They will no longer be able to share the ignorance of George Calderon's undergraduate in *The Adventures of Downy V. Green: Rhodes Scholar at Oxford*:

'I would give a thousand dollars,' said Downy, 'to have been up here with Newman . . .'

'Which Newman do you mean?' he asked.

'Why, Newman, sir; the Newman.'

'Do you mean W. G. Newman who fielded point, or T. P. Newman who broke the roof of the pavilion in the M.C.C. match?'

All the freshmen glared at Downy.

'Neither, sir, neither; Cardinal Newman, the eminent divine!'

'Never heard of him!' said the bold freshman, and went on with his egg.

B.W.M.
Oxford, January 1982

Chapter 1   Genesis 1801–16

'The Child is father of the Man.'   William Wordsworth

Born in February 1801, his life subsequently spanning eighty-nine years, John Henry Newman has emerged as a supreme genius set among nineteenth-century men of ideas and literature. He experienced conversion to a Protestant form of the revealed Christian religion at the age of fifteen, became a leader of the Anglican Church, converted to Roman Catholicism in 1845, was made a Cardinal of that Church in old age, and died in August 1890. Lytton Strachey in *Eminent Victorians* wrote incisively on Cardinal Manning, another convert from Anglicanism, who cruelly blotted out all memory of his deceased wife when he became a priest of the Catholic Church – he allowed her grave, beside which as an Anglican vicar he would sit and compose his Sunday sermons, to become dilapidated and overgrown. Strachey no more than touched on the reserved and hostile relationship between him and Newman. He described Newman as 'a child of the Romantic Revival, a creature of emotion and memory, a dreamer whose spirit dwelt apart in delectable mountains, an artist whose subtle senses caught, like a shower in the sunshine, the impalpable rainbow of the immaterial world'. Yet although Newman had strong appreciation of the beauties of the natural world, he was by no means a Romantic. His life was above all governed by his intellect. Strong convictions, worked out by hard thought, controlled the decisions which directed his life. His emotions were subject to his intellect. This was true when he underwent conversion in 1845 and in the years leading up to his reception into the Roman Church by Father Dominic Barberi, and in his youth when he made choices about his early religious directions. Lytton Strachey was helping to establish an early myth about the Oxford Movement Leaders, one of whom was Newman, and another John Keble, that they were enchanted if not infatuated by a romantic vision of the Middle Ages: 'At Oxford he was doomed. He could not withstand the last enchantment of the Middle Age.' Both men worked out their religious positions by scholarship and the exercise of the intellect: it was not a question of the spontaneous overflow of powerful feelings persuading them to their particular version of the love of God. Both Keble and Newman, and Pusey as well, were scholars and intellectuals: if any of the Movement's inspirers were at all romantic it was the lively, impetuous, enthusiastic Hurrell Froude, governed more by the heart than the head,

1. John Henry Newman's father, John Newman, Artist Unknown

2. Grey Court House, Ham, where Newman spent much of his childhood. He thought of it 'as paradise'. The house and grounds remained in his dreams throughout his life

than anyone else. Both Keble and Newman knew what it was like to be working curates of the Church of England, Keble in his father's Cotswold parish, Newman at St Clement's in Oxford. The hardships and ordinary preoccupations of poor parishioners left them with few illusions.

John Henry Newman was born in the City of London, at 80 Old Broad Street. His earliest diary records retrospectively 'Saturday, 21st February 1801: I was born.' The next entry is 'Thursday, 9th April: baptized' and the baptismal register reads 'John Henry, son of John Newman and Jemima his wife, was baptized April 9, 1801, by Robert Wells Curate.' The church in which this took place, St Benet Fink, has since disappeared.

Newman's parents were both religious. His father was not an enthusiast: he was broad- and open-minded, and did not give much regard to doctrinal niceties. His mother, Jemima Foudrinier, a woman of Huguenot stock, was much more strongly religious, basing her ways and faith firmly on the Bible which she encouraged her son to read. The family background was one of sound middle-class commerce. John Newman senior was a banker whose forbears had been East Anglian yeomen. His wife's ancestors were of slightly higher social standing and she brought with her a dowry which she diligently kept intact and eventually dispersed among her surviving children.

There were six children altogether. John was the eldest of the family, and Mary the youngest by almost nine years. In between came Charles, Harriett, Francis, and Jemima. His early life was spent between their

3. Dr Nicholas's School at Ealing, *c* 1809

house in Southampton Street in Bloomsbury, and Grey Court House at Ham. It was at Ham that Newman describes seeing lighted candles in the windows of his and other houses to celebrate victory in the battle of Trafalgar. Geoffrey Faber in *Oxford Apostles* stresses the importance of Ham to Newman's imagination. At his most distressed, and when he was in the grip of some desperate illness such as he suffered in Sicily in 1833, the house and gardens at Ham, their trees and shrubs, represented in his mind an idyllic landscape soothing to his troubled spirit. In a letter of 1886 he describes how it remained in his dreams throughout his life and while he was a schoolboy he thought of it 'as Paradise'.

In September 1807 the Newmans left the house at Ham for good and established themselves at Southampton Street. Newman went to Dr Nicholas's School at Ealing as a boarder on 1 May 1808. Dr George Nicholas was an enlightened teacher, an Oxford scholar from Wadham College, who ran his school on Eton lines, and believed in the dictum, *mens sana in corpore sano*. Francis Newman in his frank description of the early life of his brother – 'I cannot join any of the panegyrics on my brother; yet he was certainly a high-minded fanatic in regard to money' – noted that it was a large private school of 290 pupils, and although the learned Doctor might have been keen on games, Newman himself was not: 'I cannot remember seeing him at any play,' in spite of plenty going on, fives, football, marbles, hopscotch, patball and trapball. And although 'he did go to our bathing-pond', he never swam. Francis recorded that their

4. A letter written to his mother at the age of seven

father did insist that Newman learned to ride horses and it was in this pursuit that he found his exercise. The *Autobiographical Writings* of Newman endorse his brother's view. Written in that curious, distancing, objective style that the nineteenth century approved, Newman wrote of himself, 'As a child, he was of a studious turn, and of a quick apprehension ... He devoted to such literary exercises and to such books as came his way, a good proportion of his play time; and his school-fellows have left on record that they never, or scarcely ever, saw him taking part in any game.'

School life for Newman proceeded without any extraordinary events disturbing what John Keble described as 'the common round, the trivial task'. His diary of May 1810 describes days typical of any schoolboy at the time:

May 11 began first day
     13 took a walk by Duke of Kents
     17 bought mustard and pepper pot
     25 got into Ovid and Greek
     29 Oak Apple day
     30 fell in a ditch

As many small boys do, he flew kites, enjoyed fireworks, went to fairs and 'did no sums – could not get them to answer – ill'. Later, his diary 1813 describes:

    June   9 Speech day
          12 Dancing
          18 fine
          19 went home
          21 poney came, began haymaking
          26 other poney came
    Aug   4 went to Ham on ponies – afterwards to school
          10 had part in the Play given me
          13 made a monitor

His first Latin verses are dated 11 February 1811:

'In montem Domini altum quisque ascendere possit,
Cui cor est purum, cui manus innocuae.
(Into the lofty mountain of the Lord everyone who has a pure heart, and innocent hands may ascend.)'

His notebook is entitled 'Verse Book' and between the two words he has drawn the device of a cross below which is a sort of necklace. Later in his life, he reflected in his *Apologia pro vita sua* that this picture of a set of beads with a little cross attached bears a great resemblance to the rosary, and he supposed he must have derived the idea 'from some romance ... or from some religious picture ... I am certain there was nothing in the churches I attended, or the prayer books I read, to suggest them'.

His first school prize was Lamb's *Tales from Shakespeare*. Others were Milton's works, Cowper's 'Homer', and Denon's *Travels*.

The diaries record how he gets on well with some of his teachers, 'I and Mr Laurie very good friends. He took me up for a reward', and on another day, 'very good friends with Mr Laurie'. He writes on various themes, Learning, Luxury, Avarice. He practises his French in letters to his parents:

Ma chère Mère,
    Je vais donc avoir le plaisir de vous revoir. Nos vacances commencent le 21 de ce mois. Encore une quinzaine et Je serai avec vous!
    Monsr le Dr vous présente ses complimens. Moi, Je vous offre toute ma tendresse, permettez moi seulement de la partager entre mon père, et mes soeurs.
    J'ai l'honneur d'être avec joie et esperance Ma chère Mère,
        Votre très respectueux Fils,
        Jean Henri Newman.

5. At school he founded a secret society with some friends and became its leader. A caricature of the Spy Club with Newman in the chair, drawn by one of its enemies

He takes music lessons and learns the violin. The violin was to provide him with much diversion and enjoyment for the rest of his life. Francis tells how Newman and Copleston, the Provost of Oriel, 'enjoyed the violin together' when they were both in residence at College; and at the end of his life at the Birmingham Oratory, he still played his beloved violin.

Dr Nicholas's school gave him the opportunity to follow his own designs. His diaries show that he both acted and took part in debates. He also established school newspapers based on Addison's *Spectator*. He called his, *Spy* and *Beholder*. He founded a secret society with some friends and became its leader. This society did not prove too popular with many of his contemporaries, who forced an entry into one of its meetings and broke it up. In a way, though, 'the child is father of the man', and as his

brother Charles said, John 'coveted to be a Grand Master of some Order'.
These were words of prophecy indeed.

His attentions at school were taken up with other things than games. He
studied hard: 'He attempted original compositions in prose and verse
from the age of eleven, and in prose showed a great sensibility and took
much pains in matters of style. He devoted to such literary exercises and to
such books as came in his way, a good portion of his play-time.' Thus, his
Autobiographical Writings describe his school-days. He read widely and soon
took up, and fell under the influence of, two Scotts – Sir Walter and
Thomas Scott. In 1871 he wrote, 'As a boy, in the early summer mornings,
I read "Waverley" and "Guy Mannering" in bed, when they first came
out, before it was time to get up; and long before that – I think when I was
eight years old – I listened eagerly to "The Lay of the Last Minstrel",
which my mother and aunt were reading aloud.' He shared his devotion of
Sir Walter Scott with his fellow leader of the Oxford Movement, John
Keble, who in his lectures as Professor of Poetry at Oxford, considered
Scott a 'Primary Poet', and regretted that he should have given up writing
poetry because he, Scott, felt Byron was a better poet. Keble thought Scott
should have been the poet of the Church and called him the 'Scotch
Pindar'. Byron, unrestrained, arrogant and lacking in reserve, was far
from primary rank and did not live up to Scott's excellence as the 'noblest
of all poets in our own day'. These views Newman shared.

The other Scott to whom Newman paid tribute was Thomas Scott of
Aston Sandford. He admired, in Scott's history and writings, 'his bold
unworldliness and vigorous independence of mind'. The *Apologia* records
that 'when I was an undergraduate, I thought of making a visit to his
Parsonage in order to see a man whom I so deeply revered'. Thomas Scott
gave to his writing 'a minutely practical character', and Newman used as
proverbs what he thought embraced the scope and issue of his doctrine
'Holiness before Peace', and 'Growth [is] the only evidence of life'.

His most influential teacher at Ealing was the Rev. Walter Mayers of
Pembroke College, Oxford. He encouraged Newman to read a great deal
and inspired him with conversation and sermons. Mayers was 'the human
means of this beginning of divine faith in me', on account of all the books
which he put into Newman's hands, many of them Calvinistic in character. He read Romaine, Thomas Scott and many others: Jones of Nayland,
Joseph Milner's *Church History*, Newton on the prophecies, Law's *A Serious
Call to a Devout and Holy Life* and the Early Church Fathers, certainly St
Augustine and St Ambrose.

From early childhood, he had read the Bible and unaccountably he was
superstitious in a religious way. It was as though he had assimilated,
without any conscious effort or attention, religious influences of which he

was unaware. He talked about his imagination running on unknown influences, on magical powers and talismans. This predisposition to a firm religious conviction, combined with his precocious reading and given strength by Walter Mayers, led to what Newman called his 'inner conversion' of which 'I am still more certain than that I have hands or feet'. He dated this time as the Autumn of 1816 when he was fifteen, and in the *Apologia* stated, 'I fell under the influences of a definite creed, and received into my intellect impressions of dogma, which through God's mercy, have never been effaced or obscured.' At this time, too, he became convinced that he should lead a celibate life. He wrote in the *Apologia*, 'I am obliged to mention, though, I do it with great reluctance, another deep imagination, which at this time, the Autumn of 1816, took possession of me – there can be no mistake about the fact – viz. that it was the will of God that I should lead a single life.' He felt that his vocation would call in life for such 'a sacrifice as celibacy involved; as for instance, missionary work among the heathen, to which I had a great drawing for some years. It also strengthened my feeling of separation from the visible world, of which I have spoken above.' When the *Apologia* was published his reluctance was justified. One review was entitled 'The Boy Celibate' and charged him with a lack of 'elemental vitality'.

Newman's inner conversion was the culmination of this period in his intellectual and emotional development. As we have seen, Francis had no illusions about him. He regarded John as fanatical and considered that 'he always wanted balance'. In argument with his father, Newman defended George IV's and the Establishment's case, when George IV wanted to discard Queen Caroline. John Newman senior sympathized with Caroline, and abruptly concluded, 'Well, John! I suppose I ought to praise you for knowing how to rise in the world. Go on! Persevere! Always stand up for men in power, and in time you will get promotion.' Francis commented, 'My father had mistaken fanaticism for self-seeking.'

He was certainly not self-seeking in a material sense. Money meant little to him, except insofar as it had to be managed, and this he did well. As Francis said, 'He treated the zeal for Church Pelf with a lofty scorn.' Prestige, position and power, were perhaps even at this time, a different matter.

There is no doubt that, had he spent his early years in other circumstances and if his shaping influences had been other than what they were, he would have excelled in other fields. Francis observed that his 'fine taste and "subtlety" would have suited Chancery, and from Cicero he had learned the art of pommeling broadly enough for any Jury'.

Chapter 2   Oxford: Trinity and Oriel 1816–28

'But, to those that sought him, as sweet as summer.'
William Shakespeare *Henry VIII*

At the age of fifteen Newman was entered for Trinity College, Oxford. This came about almost by accident. In his *Autobiographical Writings*, he relates how on Saturday 14 December 1816, his father was in two minds about whether to direct the post-chaise boy to make for Hounslow or for the first stage of the road to Cambridge. In the event, his father seems to have decided on the Oxford direction persuaded by the Reverend John Mullens, then Curate of St James's Piccadilly. Newman described their arrival as follows:

When they got to Oxford, Mr Mullens at first hoped to find a vacancy for him in his own College, Exeter: but, failing in this, he took the advice of his Exeter friends to introduce him to Dr Lee, President of Trinity, and at that time Vice-Chancellor, by whom Newman was matriculated as a commoner of that society.

Dr Nicholas, back at Ealing, was more than satisfied. 'Trinity? A most gentlemanlike College; I am much pleased to hear it.'

He did not take up residence at Trinity until June 1817, just as all the other undergraduates were going down. He spent the intervening time reading and preparing himself for college life, although during the first half of 1817 his eyesight was very bad, 'I was not allowed or able to read much.' According to his study-diary after 18 March he read for about six hours a day, increasing the time to about nine or ten hours a day when full term started in October. The diary records the occasional half hour of violin practice as well.

Walter Mayers had given him Bishop Beveridge's *Private Thoughts upon Religion* and *Private Thoughts upon a Christian Life*. Newman replied, in a letter of thanks for the kind present, that he hoped he would 'continue firm in the principles, in which you, Sir, have instructed me, and may that Holy Spirit by whom Bishop Beveridge was enabled to establish his articles of faith ... steer me safe through the dangers, to which I may be exposed at College, or afterwards in my course through life ...'.

His tutor at Trinity was to be Thomas Short who was able to inform Newman in early June that 'a set of borrowed apartments' was vacant and at his service. Soon after Newman's arrival in Oxford, and after a visit to the tailor's to be fitted out with cap and gown, Short called Newman to him to explain some of the college customs. The commoner sent to summon him explained to Newman that Short was very strict: 'All wish

6. The interior of Trinity College Chapel. Newman became an undergraduate of the
College in 1817 and first received Communion in the Church of England in the chapel

Ingram were Tutor still.' Newman's serious cast of mind expressed
immediate preference for Short rather than the lenient Mr Ingram. Someone who was unusually reading for six hours a day looked forward to the
demands made on him by a strict tutor.

The impression of his first dinner in college is recorded in a letter to his father:

At dinner I was much entertained with the novelty of the thing. Fish, flesh and fowl, beautiful salmon, haunches of mutton, lamb etc., and fine, very fine (to my taste) strong beer, served up on old pewter plates, and misshapen earthenware jugs. Tell Mama there are gooseberry, raspberry, and apricot pies. And in all this the joint did not go round, but there was such a profusion that scarcely two ate of the same joint.

Such was the opulence of the meal. Provisions were different from those he was used to at home: 'Tell Harriett I have seen the fat cook. The wine has this moment come in. $8\frac{1}{3}$ per cent is taken off for ready money. Two things I cannot get, milk and beer so I am obliged to put up with cream for the one and ale for the other.' His mother was naturally anxious at leaving her son in unfamiliar surroundings: 'I certainly felt uncomfortable at leaving you for the first time alone in the world, but more from the fear of your feelings on the occasion, as I could not but imagine it must be a part of the Tutor's business to put the fresh students into a right train. I think you stood the *foreign* attack capitally.'

Apart from preliminary study, Newman's time was taken up in a number of other ways. Walter Mayers gave him a commission asking him to go to 'Hitchings the Tailor and request him to make me a pair of mixture pantaloons as before by Monday'. He took drinks with an under-graduate called Hollis. He was invited by some of his fellow undergradu-ates for a glass of wine 'and they drank and drank all the time I was there'. He reported that he was not entertained by either their drinking or their conversation, so that not much was to be missed by absence of their company. He commented that his first impressions were these: 'I really think, if anyone should ask me what qualifications were necessary for Trinity College, I should say there was only one – drink, drink, drink.' He took walks around Oxford, as the young gentlemen of Oxford gradually disappeared at the end of their term to various places for vacation. He found Oxford climatically a city of extremes: 'Oxford is such a flat that the wind blows down upon it and the sun scorches it, when in other places there are gentle gales and pleasant sunshine.'

Newman tried, too, to get some direction for his reading. Short had departed for the vacation already and Newman resorted to the President who said that he 'left all such questions, as Mr Newman asked, to be answered by the Tutors'. On Sunday 29 June, the day before Newman was to leave Oxford, returning from a walk in the Parks he saw one of the college tutors in top-boots riding on horseback. He stopped him and rather abruptly asked him what books he should read during the vacation.

Newman was referred to one of the tutors still in college and was in the end happily given a list.

Meanwhile the painters and decorators had moved in to renovate for the new term. Newman commented, 'While I was out today, some men who are painting throughout the College, have painted my windows, and I am nearly sick with the smell.' In a letter to his father at this time, he remarked how few people were still left in college and how he often dined by himself:

The other day I had a nice dinner set before me of veal cutlets and peas, so much to myself that I could hear the noise I made in chewing through the empty hall; till at length one came in, and sat opposite to me, but I had not been introduced to him, and he could not speak to me. Consequently, we preserved an amicable silence, and conversed with our teeth.

One of the undergraduates who left for the vacation almost as soon as Newman arrived, but not before Newman had met him and been pleased with his acquaintance, was J. W. Bowden, three years older, who was to become Newman's closest friend throughout his student days, and who was later, as a layman, to contribute to the publications of the Oxford Movement. Francis Newman was to describe him later as an extremely handsome man: 'Perhaps he was too tall for Apollo, but his modest sweetness of expression seemed Christian beauty such as I had not seen in the British Museum from any Greek.' Together, Newman and Bowden enjoyed Oxford. Newman worked hard to keep up with Bowden who was a year ahead in his studies. They took the cold plunge-baths in Holywell. They collaborated in the composition of a narrative poem *St. Bartholomew's Eve*, a romance which was received with enthusiasm and admiration by the Newman family. It was anti-Roman Catholic, the French sort in particular:

'Mistaken worship! Where the priestly plan
In servile bondage rules degraded man.'

The villain of the piece is a perfidious priest, according to Newman later in his life, inappropriately called Clement. Among other dastardly deeds, he is responsible for massacres and for leading a nightly band of assassins. Newman said that he wrote the theological parts, while Bowden composed the historical and lyrical sections; but in Meriol Trevor's judgement 'Bowden wrote the dull descriptions and Newman the dramatic episodes'.

His best friends from his Ealing schooldays were Hans Hamilton and Frederick Thresher. Hamilton went to Trinity College, Dublin and Thresher went to the Queen's College at Oxford. Newman continued to correspond with Hamilton, and a letter from Hamilton describes the nostalgia experienced for the old Ealing and Southampton Street days: 'Oh! how happy we were then; and I hope we shall both be so still. Thresher may with my full consent read any part of this letter.' Eventually, Hamilton and Thresher both became barristers, the former staying in Ireland and the latter in England. It was Bowden who remained very close to Newman until his death in 1844.

Newman's early impressions of Trinity as the most bibulous of institutions were to be further borne out. At Trinity word got about that he was adept on the violin. He received an invitation to a wine party which stressed that he would be so much the more welcome if he brought his instrument. He was introduced as 'Mr Newman and his fiddle', and 'was offered a chair, a glass and a decanter'. It is clear from Newman's account that the object of the evening was to get Newman drunk: there was little interest in his violin-playing. An hour passed:

I finished my third glass, and begged E's leave to depart. E requested silence and asked me to speak (my wishes). I did so. 'No' assailed me on every side. My voice was drowned, but they could not prevent my moving.

The studious Newman was disturbed by more impetuous youths at other times, ones that would rush into his room without knocking, bolt the door and proclaim that they were hiding from someone. They would press him to drink wine with them, and tease him about his ambitions to take a first-class degree. On one such occasion, he remonstrated with a group of intruders that their behaviour was not 'the conduct of gentlemen'. One hefty fellow, '6 feet 3 or 4 inches high, and stout in proportion', said that he would knock Newman down, had he not been so contemptible a fellow. However, the following day the great lout returned to apologize saying that 'a sudden gust of passion had overset him'.

For the most part he was not the butt of his fellow-collegians, and was able to concentrate on his studies. As he reported to his mother, his tutor Mr Short lent him a book on Mathematics including a dissertation on Euclid, and Newman busied himself with 'the multiple superparticular, sub-multiple sub-superparticular, sub-superpartient of the less inequality' and many other aspects of Euclidian theory.

The hard work proceeded with Algebra in the vacations, and he reported to his mother in February 1818, 'I went to give in my Collection-papers, namely five books of Herodotus, Virgil's Aeneid, Mechanics, and the Pentateuch, Joshua, Judges, and Ruth.'

Thomas Short suggested that he should sit for the annual scholarship examination, so impressed was he by Newman's hard work and progress. Short had been largely responsible for opening the scholarship examination to all-comers and Newman reported that the competition for £60 a year for nine years and the scholar's gown, was between the following candidates: 'five in-college men, and six out-college, viz. one from Exeter, one from Merton, two from Worcester – one from Rugby, and one not of the University'. The result was to be announced on Trinity Monday 1818, the day of the Trinity College Gaudy, the annual college celebration and dinner, when the election of Fellows and scholars was made.

Newman had no relish for such occasions which he described as grand drinking bouts, and which were not confined to Trinity: 'Such orgies, ordinary as well as extraordinary, might be called the rule of the place.' Oriel was commonly satirized for taking an austere line and imposing on its undergraduates tea instead of wine.

The news that he scarcely dared hope for came, and his diary entry reads: 'Monday 18 May 1818 elected Scholar of Trinity.' He noted himself in his *Autobiographical Writings*, 'The Trinity scholarship thus unexpectedly gained, was the only academical distinction which fell to the lot of Mr Newman during his undergraduate course.' The family was overjoyed. Francis was first to send news home by letter. His mother presented him with a twelve-volume set of *The Works of Francis Bacon*.

For many days afterwards, Newman could not believe his success. The examination had been gruelling, 'They first made us do some verses – then some Latin translation – then a Latin theme – then a chorus from Euripides – then an English theme – then some Plato, then some Lucretius, then some Xenophon, then some Livy. Most of the Latin and Greek we had to construe off to them.' Even his closest, and most intimate friend Bowden had lacked confidence in him. Newman's age was against him for a start: he was very young. Bowden thought his case desperate and, as Newman said, 'betted against me'.

As a scholar, at the end of May, he sat his first University examination, Responsions, and passed with credit, his examiner being Edward Hawkins with whom he was to become closely associated.

His mother congratulated him on his assiduity so well rewarded and it proved a virtue which was to continue throughout his undergraduate career. He wrote to Hans Hamilton in 1821 that during the Long Vacation of 1819 'I read nearly at the rate of nine hours a day. From that time till my examination in November 1820, it was almost one continued mass of reading ... during twenty out of the twenty-four weeks immediately preceding my examination, I fagged at an average of more than twelve hours a day. If one day I read only nine, the next I read fifteen.' There were, of course, other diversions. He and Bowden edited a pompous magazine called *The Undergraduate*, which sold well but probably not for the intended reasons. It generally got about that Newman was editor; for some reason Bowden's name was not publicly associated with it. This caused some embarrassment and the two resigned the periodical into the hands of the publisher. He wrote to his mother, a passage revealingly deleted from his autograph, that 'I hope we have completely weathered the storm. You would say we were admirable actors, if you saw how we behaved before people, so cool, so collected, so indifferent.' This public deception and denial of his rôle in the affair, was naturally something of which he was not proud in later years, but which was quite understand- able in the behaviour of a young student when the men of Magdalen were putting it about universally that 'Newman of Trinity is the author of *The Undergraduate*'.

The composition with Bowden of *St. Bartholomew's Eve* also provided diversion. Yet literary exploits did not deter him from his major academic tasks, and there can be no doubt that Newman overworked both in vacations and term time for his final exams.

The result was a catastrophe. Trinity had an extremely poor reputation in the final examinations. There had been no first classes in the past ten years. Newman told Walter Mayers, 'Five of us were going up for first classes this time; one has deferred his examination; one most likely goes up for no honours at all; one is expected to fail; one, whom I think quite certain of success, may before the examination remove to another College; – one remains.' On 1 December 1820 Newman wrote to his father, 'It is all over; and I have not succeeded. The pain it gives me to be obliged to inform you and my mother of it I cannot express.'

It was a terrible nemesis, especially when so much had been expected of him. He feared much more from failure than he hoped from success, and complained of those who, not knowing him, formed high expectations of him and wrote him down in advance a double first. Those who knew him similarly thought he would do well. Bowden, who had a little earlier finished his finals and obtained a second class in Mathematics, wrote from home, 'By the time you receive this, I conclude you will have completed your labours in schools, and covered yourself and the College with glory.' When the result list came out, Newman's name did not appear on the Mathematical side at all, and in Classics it was in the lower division of the second class, known contemptuously as being 'under-the-line'. So much for the double first.

There were a number of reasons for this failure. Newman had over- worked himself to a state of mental exhaustion. He was called in front of the examiners a day before he expected. He became so depressed that he had to retire from the examination schools, but not before he had made sure of gaining some sort of degree. Above all, Trinity was not one of the small clique of colleges set in the new tradition of proper academic study. Later Newman prepared a letter for publication in the Catholic

University's *University Gazette* in 1855, but which he withheld because it would have caused pain to his old Oxford tutors, John Wilson, Thomas Short, and J. A. Ogle who was to become Regius Professor of Medicine. He published it finally in *Autobiographical Writings*. It showed the deficiencies of Trinity's teaching, 'I had as little tutorial assistance or guidance as is easy to conceive.' Close supervision was not the tradition, and the idea of it was new, as Newman was to show in his own explication of ideas for a University. Only a few Colleges had cultivated study and scholarship. As he said, 'They alone had real tutors ... the teaching and the honours of the place were in the possessions of a small clique; if any one of their pupils appeared for examination, a prestige went with him.' If you were an undergraduate at one of the few, the system ensured that, as Newman put it, 'success was three-quarters certain before he had answered a question'.

Fortunately Newman's Trinity scholarship had not expired. He could continue in Oxford for several years. His parents sensibly and kindly supported him. His mother wrote that, despite his failure, everybody who knew him recognized his merit. She wrote, 'You must wait patiently and cheerfully the time appointed for your reaping the benefit of your steady assiduities.'

Newman returned to Oxford in 1821 with the intention of taking private pupils and later introducing his brother Francis to university life. His father had intended Newman for the Bar and a subsequent legal or political career. In 1819 he had been entered at Lincoln's Inn. Newman's failure in the examination schools and his increasing religious convictions enabled him to persuade his father to sanction the prospect of Newman taking Orders.

Life in Oxford continued well enough for him and his mind recovered its old enquiring habit. He attended all sorts of lectures, became interested in Anatomy and Mineralogy, and he attended concerts. On one occasion he had to leave a concert because of an uncomfortable cough. Then as now, medicine was a matter of trial and error. Newman wrote to his mother, 'Everyone prescribes something different. Dr Ogle a "linctus" or jam made of Ros. Canin. Oxymel. Tolu. Ipecac. Opium etc. The Dean a mixture of Tolu, Squills, and Paregoric in barley water. Another prescribes antimony and squills – another Ipecacuanha, Squills and Rhubarb in 24 pills, 3 at night, and 3 in the morning. However, between them all, I certainly find my cough better.'

In the middle of June 1821 Newman found himself turned out of College and he took lodgings at Seale's Coffee House. There were two sets of rooms available which proved most suitable for the advent of Francis to Oxford. In September at home a fierce argument took place which showed the strength of religious convictions in the household. On the last Sunday

7. A one pound note issued by the bank in which Newman's father was a partner until 1816

of the month Newman was called downstairs to give his opinion whether he thought it a sin to write a letter on a Sunday. Newman wrote, 'I found dear Francis had refused to copy one. A scene ensued more painful than any I have experienced.' Frank, like Newman himself, brought up under the evangelical Walter Mayers, opposed his father on this issue and Newman took his side. It is interesting to note that later Frank derided the description of Mayers as a high Calvinist: 'Like most Evangelicals of my youth, his Calvinism consisted in this, that he did not explain away the 17th Article of Predestination and Election, but bowed under it with revered shuddering.'

In October Newman wrote a letter to his father thanking him for £15 sent and saying that he would not require any more that term. He was receiving money both from his scholarship and from private pupils. It was in fact the last sum he cost his father. In November, Mr Newman was declared bankrupt. He had been a banker until 1816, when he had taken over a brewery at Alton in Hampshire: it was this financial venture that finally failed in 1821. His love, support, and generosity were so much appreciated by Newman that he always tried to keep his father's failures from public knowledge. The man who had given so much of himself for his children was not to be subjected to public humiliation.

Gradually the workings of Newman's mind made him want to recover his academic position. No one doubted his true ability: in this sense his confidence was not undermined. He finally decided on an ambitious and audacious plan, to stand for a Fellowship at Oriel. His own refusal, backed up by the opinions of others, to accept that his failure in his final exams was the true measure of his intellect, prompted him to put himself forward. Nevertheless it is true to say that in the calmness of judgement, free from the excitement and exhilaration of ambition, he thought his attempt hopeless; and it certainly startled his friends.

This time in Newman's life was difficult for him in emotional and moral terms. His journals show that he was not untouched by the preoccupations and temptations of ordinary men. Early on he had espoused chastity as an ideal way of life, but this did not mean that he was unassailed by physical or psychological temptations. There was a constant struggle against 'bad thoughts', against pride, ambition, self-esteem, and self-deception. His father often spoke as his conscience and offered a moral guide which clearly marked itself on Newman's mind. After Church on Sunday 6 January 1822, his father warned:

You poured out texts in such quantities. Have a guard. You are encouraging a nervousness and morbid sensibility, and irritability, which may be very serious. I know what it is myself, perfectly well. I know it is a disease of mind. Religion when carried too far, induces a softness of mind. You must exert yourself and do everything you can. Depend upon it no one's principles can be established at twenty.

He went on to criticize the *Christian Observer* to which Newman contributed. He branded it 'humbug' and told Newman that the letter he had written to it 'was more like the composition of an old man, than of a youth just entering life with energy and aspirations'. Obviously, there were many personal faults to watch out for.

Later that same week Mr Newman advised that Newman should make up his mind about what he was to be, 'so I chose: and determined on the Church'. Newman's diary reads: 'Friday 11th January 1822 made up my mind to go into Orders.'

In February 1822 Newman called on the Provost of Oriel and asked permission to stand for the Easter election of Fellows. Oriel was held to be pre-eminent intellectually in Oxford. In the first half of the nineteenth century it had the reputation that Jowett's Balliol was to have later on. To his father he played down his attempt:

I have no chance, and simply stand for the sake both of knowing the nature of the examination for the sake of *next* year, and being known to the examiners.

He prayed for humility of spirit: his journal for his twenty-first birthday, 21 February 1822 reads, 'Thou seest how fondly, and I fear idolatrously, my affections are set on succeeding at Oriel. Take all hope away, stop not an instant, O my God, if so doing will gain me Thy Spirit.' At the same time, he could report after calling on James Tyler of Oriel, 'I do not know how it happens – but I certainly feel very confident with respect to Oriel, and seem to myself to have a great chance of success.' Mrs Newman continued her motherly duty of boosting his confidence, 'To show you I do not think you *too old* for a Mother's correction and advice, I shall not hesitate to tell you I see one great fault in your character, which alarms me very much ... your fault is want of self-confidence, and a dissatisfaction with yourself, that you cannot exceed the bounds of human nature.' It may be that Newman's outward uncertainty hid his true feelings about the approaching contest. Mrs Newman encouraged him nonetheless and when the examinations occurred, his papers written in the first three days so impressed the Oriel Fellows that three went over to Trinity to enquire about his antecedents and general character. Thomas Short, too discreet to tell Newman the purpose of their visit, invited Newman to join him at an early dinner of lamb chops and fried parsley, and communicated his excitement by keenly encouraging him to go on confidently with the contest. This incident was important to Newman, giving him inspiration and reassurance. The result was that on Friday 12 April he was elected Fellow of Oriel.

Newman recorded in his *Autobiographical Writings* that the Provost's butler, as tradition held, called on Newman at his lodgings to deliver the news of his election. He found Newman playing the violin, and disconcerted at having to interrupt him said he had 'disagreeable news to announce, viz., that Mr Newman was elected Fellow of Oriel, and that his immediate presence was required there'. Newman responded, 'Very well', and went on fiddling. As Newman recorded, 'This led the man to ask whether perhaps he had not mistaken the rooms and gone to the wrong person, to which Mr Newman replied that it was all right. But, as may be imagined, no sooner had the man left, than he flung down his instrument, and dashed downstairs with all speed to Oriel College.' As Frank wrote to his father, 'I believe this is almost a solitary instance of an under-the-line man getting into Oriel. John is in very good health.'

That evening of 12 April he took his seat in Oriel Chapel and sat next to John Keble at dinner who appeared to him more like an undergraduate than the first man in Oxford, 'so perfectly unassuming and unaffected in manner'. Keble had been the second man in Oxford to take a double first, that is a first-class degree in both Mathematics and Classics. The first had been Robert Peel, and Keble was held to have out-Peeled Peel.

Newman met the Oriel Fellows and realized from now on he would have to call them familiarly, 'Hawkins', 'Tyler', and so on. He received the congratulations of these men of distinction and wrote to Bowden that, 'I bore it till Keble took my hand and then felt so abashed and unworthy the honour done me that I seemed desirous of quite sinking into the ground.' He saw himself now as a member of 'the School of Speculative Philosophy in England', which Oriel had been dubbed by the *Edinburgh Review*, and considered 'it is not the least advantage, that, I have, whenever I wish, the advice and direction of the first men in Oxford'.

His friend Thresher pointed out to him by letter that he had achieved one of the ambitions coveted by half the B.A.s of Oxford. He previewed the possibilities of Newman's career:

'In Holy Orders, taking pupils in College, and having a Curacy within a short distance, then Public Tutor, Vicar of —, Provost, Regius Professor of Divinity, Bishop of—, Archbishop of Canterbury. Or shall we say thus, – student-at-law, Barrister, Lord Chancellor, or at least Lord Chief Justice of the King's Bench, which of these ladders is it your intention to climb? You now have it in your power to decide.'

To his aunt Elizabeth, he attributed his whole success to God: 'I glory in confessing it was God and God alone who accomplished it . . . it was the work of Providence.' He told her that he had not been attending either to Mathematics or the Classics in the last year. None of which was perhaps quite honest; but then this letter was a condoling homily to an aunt who had suddenly found herself in debt.

At the beginning of his Oriel career, Richard Whately was the most influential man Newman came into contact with. Whately had recently given up his Fellowship on account of marriage but was still living in Oxford, certainly a powerful and important man so far as Oriel was concerned. Newman the new Fellow, on probation for a year, was entrusted to his care: Whately acted as a sort of moral tutor. Newman wrote, 'If there was a man easy for a raw bashful youth to get on with it was Whately', and he added humorously and perceptively that Whately was 'a great talker, who endured very readily the silence of his company'. He was at that time one of Oxford's outstanding characters. Thomas Short described him as 'an exceedingly rude fellow. He'll think nothing of telling you to your face that he thought you a fool. But then he was exceedingly magnanimous. He didn't mind your telling him that you thought him a fool.' Some of his personal habits were not particularly endearing: again Short told how Whately used to spit into the fire, 'I myself have seen him expectorate over his shoulder in the Corpus Common Room, wipe his mouth with his fingers, and then plunge them into a dish of almonds and raisins.' Whately told his colleagues that he was always pleased to take cubs in hand and lick them into shape, young men 'who like dogs of the King Charles's breed, could be held up by one leg without yelling'.

8. Richard Whately, Fellow of Oriel, Principal of Alban Hall, Archbishop of Dublin. Friend and mentor of Newman during his first years at Oriel. Artist unknown

9. Edward Bouverie Pusey by George Richmond. Newman said of him, 'He is humility itself, and gentleness, and love, and zeal, and self devotion.'

Newman's association with Whately lasted until 1831 when Whately was promoted to the Archbishopric of Dublin: he did not invite Newman to join him. By this time their theological positions were considerably different, and sympathy between the two grew less and less. An irreparable breach in their friendship was made in 1836 when Whately strongly disapproved of Newman's part in the campaign against Dr Hampden being appointed to the Chair of Divinity.

The year after Newman's election as Fellow, another important association was formed when Edward Bouverie Pusey was elected to Oriel. Newman found in him a kindred spirit and someone he could talk closely and confidingly to. In *Autobiographical Writings* Newman noted for 2 May 1823, 'I walked with Pusey today; indeed I have had several conversations with him on religion . . . Thank God, how can I doubt his seriousness? His very eagerness to talk of the Scriptures seems to prove it.' In the following few years Pusey was often Newman's walking companion in and around Oxford. Their intimacy, intellectually and spiritually, developed and increased. In March 1824 Newman recorded in his journal for Monday 15 March, 'Took a walk with Pusey – discoursed on Missionary subjects. I must bear every circumstance in continual remembrance. We went along

10. The old St Clement's Church, Oxford, taken down in 1829, from the drawing by F. Mackenzie engraved for the *Oxford Almanack* for 1837. It was rebuilt nearby. Newman became curate in 1824 and was the 'guarantee to subscribers that St Clement's would be active in the fight against folly and evil.'

the Lower London road, crossed to Cowley, and coming back just before we arrived at Magdalen Bridge turnpike, he confessed to me, ... O Almighty Spirit, what words shall I use? My heart is full. How should I be humbled to the dust! What importance I think myself of! my deeds, my abilities, my writings! whereas he is humility itself, and gentleness, and love, and zeal, and self-devotion. Bless him with Thy fullest gifts, and grant me to imitate him.' So began and matured another important friendship which was to be crucial for the genesis of what has come to be known as the Oxford Movement.

Newman's decision was that he should take Holy Orders. In May 1824 he was offered and accepted the curacy of St Clement's Church in Oxford. The incumbent, John Gutch, was old and incapacitated. It had been decided to rebuild the church, and the engagement of a curate was to be a guarantee to subscribers that St Clement's would be active in the fight against folly and evil: '... every exertion will be made, when the Church is built, to recover the parish from meeting houses, and on the other hand alehouses, into which they had been drawn from want of convenient Sunday worship.' He considered that the parish of 1500 souls was increasing 'and likely to give much trouble'. He regarded the only objection to his taking the position to be his 'weakness of voice'. On Sunday 13 June he was ordained Deacon in Christ Church. He felt his heart shudder as the Bishop's hands were laid on him: 'The words "for ever" are so terrible', he wrote, 'I feel as a man thrown suddenly into deep water.'

The pastoral work at St Clement's was arduous. He visited the sick and kept notes. He went about raising subscriptions for the new building, and collected over five thousand pounds. Pusey paid for the church gallery which could accommodate at least ninety-five children whom Newman had gathered for a catechism class.

At this time Edward Hawkins, a Fellow of Oriel when Newman had been elected, was Vicar of St Mary's, the University Church. He had been made Vicar in 1823. Newman got on well with Hawkins and throughout a couple of Long Vacations when both stayed in Oxford, they grew to know each other well. Hawkins was another great influence on Newman. He criticized his sermons and made Newman aware of the moulding force of history and tradition on the development of ideas. Hawkins had preached a sermon on tradition which had caused a stir of religious feelings at St Mary's in 1818. He also made a serious assault on Newman's evangelical position when he read the draft of Newman's first sermon.

Walter Mayers now had the living of Over Worton in Oxfordshire. Newman was to stand in for Mayers on Sunday 25 July 1824. The text for his first sermon was, 'Man goeth forth to his work and to his labour until the evening.' Nineteen years later he took the same text for his last sermon preached in the Anglican Communion. Newman showed his first sermon to Hawkins who, although there was only twelve years difference in their ages, often acted in a rôle more like that of tutor to his pupil, rather than that of friend to friend. Mayers had invited Newman to preach on behalf of the starving silk-weavers of Spitalfields, a cause on which many charity sermons were concentrating. Hawkins saw at once that the tone was evangelical and that it implied a denial of baptismal regeneration: he criticized it immediately on this score: the world cannot be divided into two distinct classes, one all darkness, the other light: no such line of demarcation can be drawn across any body of men. Hawkins held that men are not either saints or sinners but that, as Newman came to see and to expound, 'they are not so good as they should be, and better than they might be'. He advised that preachers should follow the example of St Paul, who did not divide his brethren into two, the converted and the unconverted, but 'addressed them all as "in Christ", "sanctified in Him", and as having had "the Holy Ghost in their hearts"; and that while he was rebuking them for irregularities and scandals'. Hawkins gave Newman a copy of Archbishop Sumner's *Apostolical Preaching* which Newman later paid tribute to in his *Autobiographical Writings*, 'This book was successful in the event beyond anything else, in routing out evangelical doctrines from Mr Newman's Creed.' With two ideas, that of the principle of history and tradition, and that of the example of apostolical preaching, Hawkins was

11. Edward Hawkins, Fellow of Oriel, from a painting by Sir Francis Grant. He preceded Newman as Vicar of St Mary's, Oxford, until he became Provost of Oriel College. He made a serious assault on Newman's evangelical position

responsible for embarking Newman on his shift away from evangelical doctrines.

Frank was exasperated by Newman's moves away from evangelicalism. He wrote in his account of the early years of Newman that he was shocked when he found that the central doctrine of the preached sermon was that all the baptized, and only the baptized, are Christians. The manuscript argument which he had read took a different evangelical view. He could not understand what accounted for the change in emphasis. The answer lay in the influence of Hawkins.

In the same account Frank took Newman to task about the Virgin Mary. As we know from Newman's 'Chronological Notes' at the end of 1825, he lived in a succession of lodging houses from 1821 to 1826, in a house opposite Balliol, at Seale's Coffee House, at Palmer's, Messenger's, Varney's, and Combe's. During much of the time Frank was with him. Frank noted that while he was arranging furniture in his new rooms in 1824 he found a beautiful engraving of the Blessed Virgin fixed on the wall. He requested the print shop to remove it but was told it had been ordered by Newman. He remonstrated with his brother, 'But after *my* repulse of his engraved Virgin, he came out with an attack on *Protestants Collectively*, saying that they forgot that sacred utterance "Blessed art thou among women".' Frank detected in Newman the view that the New Testament was incomplete without tradition, and so far as the Invocation of the Virgin was concerned Frank declared: 'The sad importance of this to me was clear when in 1827 I went to Ireland, and saw popular Catholic manuals. From them I concluded, he had pilfered his arguments.'

He went on to pull Newman up on his statement in the *Apologia* that Hurrell Froude had fixed deep in him the idea of devotion to the Blessed Virgin: 'But J.H.N. knew him only in 1826. Is not this inconsistent with my statement about her in 1824?' Whatever the facts, it is certain that Newman was on the move away from the evangelical position when he preached his maiden sermon in 1824.

As curate of St Clement's his time was busily taken up visiting, christening, marrying and burying, writing sermons and preaching. In September 1824 his father fell ill, and Newman went to London to be with him and the family. On 29 September his father died: the corpse was laid out, 'He looked beautiful, such calmness, sweetness, composure, and majesty were in his countenance. Can a man be a materialist who sees a dead body? I had never seen one before.'

Responsibility for the family fell on him. Charles left the family, finding it too religious, for a Clerkship in the Bank of England, secured by Bowden. Frank was still at Oxford. Newman supplemented his income by various means, private pupils, College Offices. In October he was elected

Junior Treasurer: 'This will add £60, I believe, to my income.'

At the end of November Richard Heber, one of the founders of the Athenaeum Club earlier that year, sent Newman a list of members for his inspection and said that he would propose his name to the Committee for election without ballot if he wished it. Newman noted, 'I declined'.

The following March Whately was inducted as Principal of Alban Hall and immediately offered Newman the Vice-Principalship. The following day he accepted, 'I have all along thought it was more my duty to engage in College Offices than in parochial duty. On this principle I have acted.' A typically strenuous day Newman recorded in his diary: 'Monday 18 April finished seeing men at Alban Hall – visited Munt and Brooklands (out) and Harpur – engaged (as lately) with forthcoming address about St Clem: dined in College – engaged about article for review and Junior Treasurer business.'

At the end of May he was ordained priest in Christ Church by the Bishop of Oxford. He rejoiced in the ceremony: 'What a divine service is that of Ordination! The whole has a fragrance in it; and to think of it is soothing and delightful.' He reflected that he no longer maintained that the Holy Spirit always, or generally, accompanies the act of baptism, 'only that the sacrament brings them into the Kingdom of grace'. He ascribed his change of view about the doctrine of Regeneration to his parochial work: he found most of his parishioners 'in that condition as if they had some spiritual feelings, but weak and uncertain'. He described a usual Sunday's business:

I first read morning Service at Alban Hall. Then came my duty and Sermons at St Clement's. Then the Sunday School for a while. Then churched and baptized. Then baptized privately, and visited a sick person, and, having a bad cold, I am tired. (I suppose I have left out the Sunday afternoon service by mistake.)

In 1826 matters improved financially for Newman when he was appointed Tutor of Oriel, Jelf his predecessor going to be private tutor to Prince George of Cumberland. It secured him between £600 and £700 a year, and enabled him to give up both his curacy and his Alban Hall position. At the same time his sense of the value of time increased. He wrote in his journal, 'The age I am getting quite frightens me. Life seems passing away, and what have I done? Teach me, Lord, the value of time, and let me not have lived in vain.'

The pressures on him of his various duties had been worrying him for some time: some tasks he had been neglecting for the sake of others:

I have been involved (in 1825) in work against my will. This year Smedley asked me to write an article in the Encycl. After undertaking it, Whately offered me the

Vice Principalship. The Hall accounts etc., being in disorder, have haunted me incessantly. Hence my parish has suffered. I have a continual wear on my mind, forgetting, mislaying memoranda, names etc.

Now he was able to enter on the Oriel Tutorship with a restored peace of mind at least in most things, and some new ideas.

He now rejected predestination and election in the Calvinistic sense, finding no proof of them in Scripture, and Pusey accused him of becoming more and more High Church. He continued to search his own soul over motives and recorded in his early journals appeals to God to keep himself from the sin of self-pride:

How is it I think so little to what I did, about going as a Missionary? I fear thoughts of theological fame, desire of rising in the Church etc. counteract my desire for missionary employment. What I want is a humble, simple, upright, sincere, straightforward mind. I am full of art and deceit, double dealing, display.

The academic and pastoral duties of the Tutorship were what he felt he was most suited for. He saw the Tutorship as an opportunity of doing spiritual good. Oriel undergraduates were in general profligate, men of family, and, more often than not, fortune. He thought Tutors ought to see a great deal of the men in their charge and devote part of their time to giving direct religious instruction. He did not like the practice of compulsory communion services for the College, or compulsory attendance at evening chapel, especially when preceded, or followed, by drunken parties. When he raised the issue with Copleston, the Provost, and Tyler, the Dean, neither were interested in upsetting the *status quo* of College practices. Copleston even snubbed him in Hall for hacking at a haunch of venison: as Newman perceptively noted later, that snub had little to do with his treatment of the joint, but was to show that Newman's reformist views were not supported by the College's highest authorities.

Two gratifying events occurred that year which pleased Newman particularly. Two new Fellows were elected to Oriel, Newman praying that the men chosen might be 'holy and humble men, laborious, active, and self-denying': they were Robert Wilberforce and Hurrell Froude. After initial reticences, Froude, who had been tutored by John Keble, and Newman became staunch friends and campaigners. In 1829 when Oriel was pledged as a College to support Sir Robert Peel in the General Election, they combined to organize a campaign against him which, in effect, lost him the election to Sir Robert Inglis. On Froude's death, it was Newman and Keble who edited his literary remains.

Froude was considerably different from Newman. Unlike Newman who was from a middle-class London background, and was someone struggling to support his family on his father's death, Froude was from a gentlemanly background. His father was a wealthy Archdeacon who lived at Dartington in Devon. Hurrell Froude was used to gentlemanly pursuits, riding, shooting, sailing and was lively and athletic; but when their minds met their intellects worked on each other to common benefit.

The other pleasing news for Newman was that when the degree results were published in 1826, Frank's name appeared in both first classes. He saw his own failure in the final exams as a punishment and lesson in humility: then, his gaining of a Fellowship a divine gesture that enabled him to take Frank by the hand and lead him to success.

In February 1827 Newman remarked, 'Frank is off my hands, but the rest are now heavier.' Finally, in the Autumn of 1827, he settled his mother and sisters in Brighton, first at Eastern Terrace, then later at 11 Marine Square. He preferred it to Bath, which he had been considering, and supervised everything, down to the interior decoration, himself.

His tuition at Oriel was appreciated by all those who received it. He confessed privately in his journal that he fancied his pupils had a high opinion of him. He regretted in other ways that he was becoming worldly: he was too preoccupied with thoughts about livings, the Provostship, promotions. He was beginning to neglect prayer and reading of the Scriptures.

At the same time, his Oriel companions helped to concentrate his mind on suitable subjects, and he recorded that Joseph Blanco White, a clergyman of Spanish stock much admired by Provost Copleston, and therefore made a member of Oriel Common Room, had joined 'our common room party'. Newman had known Blanco White since 1822 when he had occupied rooms in the same lodging house, Palmer's, as Newman and Frank. Frank described him as a learned priest who enjoyed arguing with Newman and playing the violin with him. He reported one of Blanco's sharp retorts, 'Ah! Newman! if you follow that clue it will draw you into Catholic error.' He thought that Blanco was warning about self-flagellation, maceration of the body and unnatural self-hatred. Newman in 1827 found Blanco White 'a very well read, ardent, ingenious, warm hearted, simple minded, pious man', and commented, 'I like him very much'.

As Newman observed in the *Apologia*, towards the end of 1827, 'I began to be known'. He was a Fellow, and a public Tutor, of Oriel, a University preacher, he had written one or two Essays which were well received, and in 1827 itself he was appointed one of the Public Examiners for the BA degree. 'It was to me like the feeling of spring weather after winter; and, if I may so speak, I came out of my shell; I remained out of it till 1841.'

The following year, 1828, was to prove even more crucial for him than any that had gone before.

Chapter 3   The Vicar of Oxford 1828–33

'Mary is the pattern of our faith.'   J. H. Newman

Francis Bacon was of this opinion: 'Young men are fitter to invent than judge, fitter for execution than counsel, and fitter for new projects than for settled business'. It was certainly true of Newman. At St Clement's his ideas about church music conflicted with the choir's and its members left. Much the same was to happen later at Littlemore when it was part of his vicariate. Visiting the houses of Littlemore in 1829–30 his brother Frank discovered much 'discontent and plentiful vexation' with the vicar. Newman had apparently decided to manage musical affairs himself. Frank wrote:

Rustic musicians, who from neighbourly kindness, in a petty church which could not afford an organ, had for years freely contributed their best skill in flute, violoncello, and two other instruments, now received instead of thanks, a slap in the face by a prohibition to play. (What was his musical substitute, I either did not hear or have forgotten.)

According to Frank, nobody was to be consulted about favourite hymns and psalms: strangely enough, past custom was to stand for nothing. His conclusion was: 'It may seem unwise to waste pen and ink on petty matters; but small things may reveal deep tendencies.' Frank's purpose in recounting Newman's early history was to detect signs that showed him capable of, and drifting towards, Roman Catholic beliefs and practices; and it must be remembered that Frank was a convinced evangelical. Newman wrote to his mother in the Autumn of 1827 alluding to Frank's emotional evangelicalism, 'but I lament to see with you that his mind is warped in one respect'. Yet even so, and bearing Frank's own bias in mind, one has to recognize an essential truth in his remarks. There is no doubt about Newman's reforming, almost revolutionary, zeal within the Church of England. When it extended to the simple folk of his parishes, people who were by no means his intellectual equals, those congregations were upset and perplexed by his new ideas.

Perhaps the name he was beginning to make for himself went slightly to his head and gave him a false sense of his own superiority over most others. This is not to say that he was not on the watch for such a fault: he was always careful to cultivate the Christian virtue of humility and often prayed in tones of self-abnegation. Yet as he said himself, he was getting

well-known. In July 1828 the Bishop of London, William Howley, later to
be Archbishop of Canterbury, informed Newman that there was a vacancy in the list of Whitehall Preachers for the second part of December,
and invited him to fill it. He accepted with grateful thanks, and duly
preached at Whitehall both morning and afternoon on Sunday 21
December and Sunday 28 December.

The early part of 1828 was taken up with Oriel College politics. Late in
1827, on 23 November, Copleston was appointed Bishop of Llandaff and
Dean of St Paul's which meant that he had to vacate the Provostship. The
talk of the Oriel Fellows was to find a successor as quickly as possible, and
soon it became clear that the contest was between Hawkins, then Vicar of
St Mary's the University Church, and Keble, a country clergyman, curate
to his father at Fairford. There was plenty of canvassing, machinations,
to-ing and fro-ing of letters. Early in December 1827, Keble wrote to his
brother Thomas, 'You see friend Cop. is really going away from Oriel, and
we are all 6's and 7's about who is to be Dr in his place, i.e., about 5 of the
fellows have signified to me their wish that I would. 3 have said as much to
Hawkins, and 5 are undeclared.' True to his nature, he early on declared
that he thought it best to thank his colleagues and say, 'Hawkins had
better be the man'; but he was persuaded to stay in the competition.

The news of Copleston's elevation coincided with Newman examining
in Schools for the BA degree. He was already worried by family business,
excited and tired by examining, and Copleston's news, as he said, 'completed my incapacity'. He dreamed, drooped and found his mind wander-
ing or vacant. He felt compelled to leave off examining and on his doctor's
advice was 'leached at the temples'. He retired to convalesce.

The election of a new Provost provoked many letters. Newman was in
favour of Hawkins as a capable man of affairs. He wrote to Keble explaining his position: 'I have lived more with Hawkins than with any other
Fellow – and have thus had opportunities for understanding him more
than others. His general views so agree with my own, his practical notions,
religious opinions, and habits of thinking, that I feel vividly and
powerfully the advantages the College would gain when governed by one
who pursuing ends to which I cordially approve would bring to the work
powers of mind to which I have long looked up with great admiration.' As
he said to H. J. Coleridge, an Oriel Fellow who later became a Jesuit, 'I
knew Hawkins and he had taken me up, while Keble had fought shy of
me.'

Others took differing views. Newman urged Robert Wilberforce to
come out in favour of Hawkins, but Wilberforce, though admitting to
Hurrell Froude that he would be more suited than Keble to 'the task of
cleansing that Augean stable – the meeting of Heads', in the end declared

for Keble: 'I have come to a conclusion in favour of Keble. I have not time to explain to you my grounds; but, to speak in short, it was the *effect*, which I remember Keble uniformly produced by all he did, both in the College and in the University.'

A retired Fellow of Oriel, J. B. Ottley, divined rightly that it was quite likely that Keble would not think the Provostship 'so conducive to his happiness as the duties and pleasures of a Parish Priest'. Pusey was in favour of Hawkins's 'great knowledge of human nature, and a general practical turn of mind'. If 'personal excellence, high talents, a pure and beautiful mind' were to determine the choice, then Keble was the man. He judged they were not and much later in 1876 at the consecration of Keble College Chapel he publicly lamented his choice, 'The whole of the later history of our Church might have been changed had we been wiser . . . To us it became a sorrow of our lives.'

Newman's opinion was firm, and he advised his colleagues that they were electing 'not an angel but a Provost'. In the event, Keble resigned from the contest in favour of Hawkins and characteristically did not hold Newman's views against him. He wrote to Newman, 'However partial one might be to oneself, your knowing so much more of Hawkins is enough to prevent anyone with a spark of commonsense in his head from being hurt at your preference of him.' At the end of January, Hawkins was elected Provost, and, as it turned out, Newman lived to have reservations about his championing of Hawkins. As time went on their views both in religious matters and on running the College differed significantly.

Keble's consolation in leaving the field to Hawkins was that he could continue to emulate the example of George Herbert's ideal country parson. It was an inverted ambition which made him feel that he was doing better in the sight of God than other men of his ability in major and more public positions. Consolation of a sort came in the knowledge, too, that *The Christian Year*, his collection of hymns and poems, published in 1827, was a success. Newman informed him that it brought comfort to his dying sister Mary. She died in January 1828 and Newman wrote to Wilberforce, 'During the whole of Saturday she was in little pain – and told us that during the acuteness of her previous spasms she had received great comfort from being able to repeat to herself Keble's hymns – And so she departed.' He repeated the information to Keble at the time of Hawkins's election, 'They were the consolation of my dear Sister during the short illness which took her from us.'

Newman's support of Hawkins initially served him well. As Copleston had to retire from the Provostship on his elevation, so Hawkins had to give up St Mary's. Who was more appropriate to fill the vacancy but one of Hawkins's chief lieutenants? On Friday 14 March Newman was

12. St Mary's, the University Church, Oxford. Newman was Vicar from 1828 to 1843

instituted by the Bishop of Oxford at St Mary's. The following Sunday he read prayers there in the morning, and Provost Hawkins read them in the afternoon. The new regime was established. The pre-eminent College of Oxford had its new Provost, St Mary's its new Vicar.

St Mary's helped to bring Newman's name to the forefront of Church affairs. Frank described how Newman often used him to call on and look after the poor people of Littlemore which was attached to the city church of St Mary. Frank saw how Newman was able to use the St Mary's pulpit

13. Newman in St Mary's Church. J. A. Froude wrote of one of the sermons he preached there: 'Newman had described closely some of the incidents of our Lord's Passion; he then paused. For a few moments there was a breathless silence. Then in a low, clear voice, of which the faintest vibration was audible in the farthest corner of St Mary's, he said, "Now I bid you recollect that He to whom these things were done was Almighty God." It was as if an electric stroke had gone through the church.'

to publicize his religious views and those which were to be the Oxford Movement's. His apparent exploitation of his position did not please Frank. He appreciated that Oriel College, as rector of the Oxford parish of St Mary, appointed its vicar, but Frank interpreted the vicar's role as pastor of the non-academical souls. It was true that the University, as a central body, had spent £3,000 in 1827 on refitting the church, and because of its generosity and patronage had acquired the right of occupying it for University sermons at times different from the parish services. Newman was supposed to preach to the local tradesmen and College servants. However, in the popular mind, both in Oxford and beyond, he was considered to be a University preacher from the pulpit of St Mary's, whose views on the state of the Church of England carried considerable weight. His standing with the clergy was enhanced. Frank reported, an old country parson who had been impressed by Newman's Tracts, as remarking in the winter of 1834–5, 'Well! though one cannot accept many things from those Tracts for the Times, I am glad to see someone at last standing up for our old Church. It is too bad to see her subjected to we know not what from Dissenters in Parliament.'

Shortly before his institution as Vicar of St Mary's, Walter Mayers had died. Newman agreed to preach the funeral sermon at Worton much to

14. Sir Robert Peel, Prime Minister 1834–5, 1841–5 and 1845–6. He was elected M.P. for Oxford University in 1817. Newman successfully opposed his re-election in 1829

Mrs Mayers's satisfaction: 'At its close that evening,' she wrote, 'I seemed to be raised far above things of time and sense. I forgot I was a mourner. The perusal of it is a constant pleasure, and, I trust, benefit. The delineation of character it portrays is most faithfully correct – and proves how much you had opportunity of examining and estimating his worth.' The man who had been one of Newman's closest counsellors since his Ealing schooldays had gone.

In effect, Newman had left Mayers's kind of Church of England Christianity some way behind, and was now developing his own religious thought in the company of other great intellects such as Keble's and Pusey's.

It was not long before Newman found himself regretting his support of Hawkins for the Headship of Oriel. Froude and Newman soon found themselves opposed to Hawkins and campaigning against him on a political issue. Sir Robert Peel was the sitting Member of Parliament for the University which in those days returned its own representative to the House of Commons. At first Peel had been against Roman Catholic emancipation, against admitting them to parliament. Gradually his views changed and when he was finally convinced that their emancipation would be best for the nation, he decided honourably to resign his seat and submit himself to his constituency for re-election.

An opponent for Peel as candidate was found in Sir Robert Inglis who despite Peel's, and the Duke of Wellington's, change of mind, still supported the exclusion of Roman Catholics from Parliament. Both Froude and Newman became leading, active members of the Inglis Committee formed to get him elected.

Newman's motives for opposing Peel were complicated. In itself, Roman Catholic emancipation was no bad thing: yet he deplored an addition to the number of people in Parliament who were not members of the Church of England but who, because of the Church being so closely allied to the State, were able to vote on decisions affecting the Church of England. There were already enough dissenters, and no doubt even atheists, in Parliament who were able to vote on issues affecting the government of the Church of England. There was also the question of whether Peel deserved to be re-elected. The man had changed his mind. Newman considered that Peel had taken the University by surprise and that, in addition, a great University like Oxford should not be bullied even by a great Duke, such as Wellington.

Hawkins and the older 'noetics', as they were known, of Oriel supported the Government and Peel, and went so far as to pledge Oriel's support to Peel. So successful was the Inglis campaign, largely because of Newman's and Froude's exertions, that Inglis gained the seat much to the annoyance of the Provost and Newman's other mentor, Whately. The latter suspected that Newman had abandoned liberalism for conservative orthodoxy out of worldly ambition and showed his displeasure by inviting Newman to dinner and seating him between two ultra-conservative Heads of Colleges, 'two-bottle-orthodox old Tories'. Newman took it all in good spirit although the conversation was not intended to sparkle, nor did it. Thomas Short told how Whately asked Newman if he were proud of his friends and concluded, 'It was the end of Whately's influence over him.'

The issue was not party political in principle, but religious. Froude, Newman and others like them saw the ideal position for the Church of England as separate and free from the state: it should be autonomous and powerful. This business did not endear either of them to Hawkins, who although of liberal views quickly decided that the Provost's position was sufficient for representing the Fellows' views to the University's governing body. Soon the younger Fellows, concerned that their views should count for so little, called him satirically 'the College'.

The real clash between Newman and Hawkins came over the responsibilities and rôle of the Tutorship. There were four College Tutors, Newman, Froude, Robert Wilberforce and Joseph Dornford. The last adhered to Hawkins's policy: the other three expounded new ideas about the Tutorships. Whately saw in Wilberforce's and Froude's allegiance to

Newman the signs of an incipient party and Newman in the *Apologia* remarked, 'And thus we discern the first elements of that movement afterwards called Tractarian.'

There were two main issues involved in the disagreement between the Tutors and Hawkins, and for a long time Dornford was united with Newman over them. The arguments began almost as soon as Hawkins assumed office in 1828 and lasted until Newman ceased his Tutorship in 1830. The first issue concerned the nature of the Tutorship which Hawkins regarded as disciplinarian rather than pastoral. Newman held that a Tutor was bound to fulfil a pastoral role towards his own group of students, 'Secular education could be so conducted as to become a pastoral cure.' Hawkins felt that Newman ran the risk of sacrificing the many undergraduates who might either be wayward or not Newman's own pupils for the few who might be serious-minded and his own pupils: it seemed a system which encouraged undue personal influence and favouritism.

At first Hawkins allowed affairs to take their course, and let the Tutors work as they would. Inevitably a break-down between the college administration and the Tutors occurred. At the beginning of 1829, the Tutors decided to act, and organize their work, according to their own view of their office, and they did not inform Hawkins because they felt they sensed that he would put his veto on their proposals. They maintained that their office was a University position and that they were answerable to the Vice-Chancellor rather than the Provost. They considered that they were entitled to draw up their lecture list, attend to their own pupils first, and other undergraduates secondly: it was enough for the Provost to be able to inspect their Lecture Table and examine their pupils on it at the end of term.

Finally Hawkins enquired about the way the Tutorships were being carried out and at the end of April 1830, Newman sent him a 'sketch of the lecture-system which has been in substance in operation since Christmas-Year'. From that time the battle was out in the open. Newman was peremptory as he admitted himself, and when he had made up his mind 'was apt to be what Isaac Williams considered irreverent and rude in the nakedness of his analysis, and unmeasured and even impatient in enforcing it'. Hawkins, strong in his own position, refused to give way. Newman admitted that he had expected great things from Hawkins's Provostship but had been deeply disappointed, 'Mr Newman might have acted more generously towards a man to whom he owed much; but he had various grievances in regard to Dr Hawkins from the time that he became Provost, which made him very sore . . .'

In the end Hawkins out-manoeuvred Newman. He stated firmly that 'if you cannot comply with my earnest desire, and feel bound therefore to say that, I shall not feel justified in committing any other pupil to your care'. Newman was forced to accept 'that on learning there were such understood principles of some years standing which he could not approve, though he did not resign because his office was an University one, he was willing to be displaced because his system was not the College one'. In effect, he acquiesced in his own quiet removal from the Tutorship: the position had at last become untenable.

At the end of this period, the Vice-Chancellor invited him to become a Select Preacher of the University. This was a mark of distinction and he accepted it promptly. It may be that this sign of favour strengthened Newman in his stand against the Provost, but undoubtedly the decision to offer him the preachership had been made some time before the climax of the Tutorship row. The appointment in any case was for a year and at the end of it and thereafter he was not asked again. During the year of his office the University authorities tried to arrange the times of his sermons outside the full University term. It was a way of making sure that he preached to as few people as possible. His views were not to be propagated.

He had other worries as well. There had been trouble over the Church Missionary Society. A pamphlet entitled *Suggestions in behalf of the Church Missionary Society* had been printed and circulated anonymously, but largely because of Frank's efforts, it was soon known that Newman was its author. His self-confessed idea was 'to enlarge the circle of subscribers to the Society, and to direct and strengthen the influence of the University and thereby the Anglican hierarchy, upon it'. This move was intensely resented by the majority of its members most of whom were evangelicals, and they saw it as a means of packing the votes. Although Newman's plans applied in the first instance only to the Oxford Bible Society, a branch of the Church Missionary Society, he clearly meant it to be extended elsewhere. He sustained a great deal of adverse criticism, not least of all from his brother Frank. He told how Samuel Rickards, once a Fellow of Oriel, then a Suffolk rector and a correspondent of Newman's, described the ridiculous position he had found himself in. He had taken it upon himself to deny Newman's authorship of the pamphlet 'because to speak plainly, it was unworthy of him, and really mean; and now comes on me the mortification of having to go round and tell people that after all they were right, and it is your brother's'. The fiasco of this pamphlet and the attempt by Newman to unseat an old established evangelical secretary of the Oxford branch led eventually to his failure to gain re-election as joint-secretary. Frank recalled that B. W. Newton, a Fellow of Exeter College, proposed that Newman should be replaced as secretary and it

15. A sketch of the Newman family by Maria Giberne, *c* 1830.
Left to right: Francis, Mrs Newman, Harriett, John Henry, Jemima

'was carried at once, and, I believe, nemine contradicente'.

Another worry was his mother's and sisters' welfare. They decided to
move nearer to him and settle in or near Oxford; but this cropped up just
when his income was about to decrease on account of his relinquishing the
Tutorship. Various cottages and houses were looked at, some tried for but
missed, and finally in October a house was secured on Rose Hill. Newman
was congratulated by his mother as being a superb manager and she
hoped that they would all be of much use to him in the Littlemore parish.
Although during 1831 he even fitted out a room for himself at Rose Hill,
they were not to stay there for long, and soon moved down to a small house
in Iffley called Rose Bank.

With the duties of the Oriel Tutorship diminishing, Newman gave a
great deal more attention to his sermons. At least he had a public platform. As both Vicar of St Mary's and Select Preacher his was, despite all
his antagonists' efforts, an important voice. Many of his sermons dwelt on
the subjects of faith and reason in Christian thought, and were to provide
some of the groundwork of his later book *An Essay in Aid of a Grammar of
Assent*. In the midst of disappointment, he was still able to find new
purpose and new direction. He still had pupils who had started with him

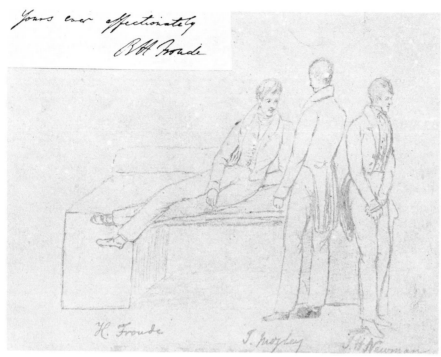

16. Hurrell Froude, Thomas Mozley and Newman in the Oriel Common Room, 1832

and were to run their course. He wrote to his mother in the summer of 1830, 'It is at length settled that the Provost gives us no more pupils – us three (Wilberforce, Froude, and me) and we die off gradually with our existing pupils'; and they all went on to do well, many of them becoming first-class graduates. Newman was never to regret his views on the nature of the tutor's relationship with his student: he was not persuaded to change his mind.

In the middle of September 1831 came the news that Whately, Principal of Alban Hall, had been appointed Archbishop of Dublin. It was a surprise. Newman enquired of Thomas Mozley, an ex-pupil and Fellow of Oriel who was later to marry Harriett, 'What think you of Whately's preferment?' Keble wrote to Newman, 'I am quite astonished at what you tell me about Whately, and can only say, I hope he and the Irish Church may be the better for it this day six months. It will be an excellent omen to that effect, if they have made no truckling bargain with him to sacrifice the temporalities to a Reformed Parliament, if such be their good pleasure.' In this way, privately, Keble sounded a warning to Parliament against interference with the Irish Church.

Almost immediately, on 29 September, exactly a week after the great Reform Bill had been passed in the House of Commons, Whately offered

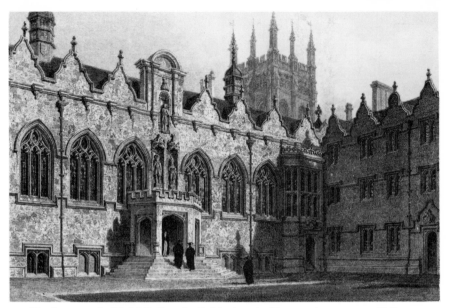

17. The front quad of Oriel College by F. Mackenzie. Newman's rooms as a Fellow were on the first floor on the right-hand side

Newman the opportunity to be Vice-Principal of Alban Hall again, since he was taking Samuel Hinds, who held the post, with him to Dublin as Archbishop's Chaplain. Newman delayed a decision, possibly because he believed he might be asked by Whately to go to Dublin as well, and possibly at the back of his mind he thought he might be asked to become Principal of Alban Hall. He eventually decided that neither possibility was acceptable. He wrote to Harriett in October that on first hearing of Whately's preferment he was annoyed lest at some time or other he would be asked to join Whately in Dublin. He felt that 'a post in Ireland was the one thing which seemed to have claims enough,' to draw him from Oxford. He saw good reasons for not going. Hugh Rose, founder of the influential *British Magazine*, had asked him to write a history of the early Councils of the Church, and he felt that in troubled times Oxford needed 'hot-headed men, and such I mean to be'. In the event, Whately never did ask him: as Newman said, 'He knew me better than I knew myself.' Nor did he become Head of Alban Hall. Rickards wrote, 'I very earnestly hope that they will put you into Whately's place, that ought to be vacant by this time.' Others saw the position as suitable for Newman, but Froude asked, 'Can it be that Hampden will succeed to the Albany?' Renn Dickson Hampden had received a substantial number of Oriel undergraduates for tuition, when Newman was no longer acceptable to Hawkins. Others realized that his Vicarship of St Mary's was just as important as anything else. Thomas Short, scouting for applicants for the tutorships and mathematical professorship at Durham University, wrote to him, 'I know you are wedded to St Mary's Church.' Meanwhile, his Oriel friends and pupils had made him a valuable gift of thirty-six volumes of the Fathers, 'among these are the works of Austin, Athanasius, Cyril Alexandrinus, Epiphanius, Gregory Nyssen ... Altogether I am now set up in the Patristical line – should I be blessed with health and ability to make use of them'. These works were fundamental for his writing from now on, and he saw them as the basis for Rose's commission on the early Councils.

Working hard at the book throughout 1831 and the first half of 1832, he finished it on 31 July. He wrote in his diary, 'Finished my work (D.G.).' In late October he recorded that he had received a letter from Rose, and one from Archdeacon Lyall to Rose, 'plucking my "Arians".' Lyall was opposed to including the book in their Theological Library series. He interpreted Newman's work as 'a History of Arianism – and presupposes so much knowledge on the part of his readers, that it is adapted only to a select class of students. The succeeding volumes, if they are to form one work with the volume as we have seen, will be a History of *Heresies*: an important subject but which is not required.' He went on, 'Mr Newman's views seem to me more favourable to the Romanist writers, than I should like to put forward in the *Theological Library*.' He concluded that he would not altogether relish his name, nor Rose's, being directly associated with the publication: he would rather recommend it to Rivington, the publisher, for separate publication. After a long time of deliberation, Rivington did take it and it appeared in 1834 as *The Arians of the Fourth Century*.

Just before the news of Lyall's criticism, Froude invited Newman to join him and his father, Archdeacon Froude, on a winter voyage to the Mediterranean. Froude was suffering from tuberculosis of the lungs and it was generally considered that a winter spent in England would be dangerous for his life. On Saturday 8 December the trio set sail from Falmouth for the Mediterranean: 'Went on board the packet (Hermes) about $\frac{1}{2}$ past 10 a.m. set off at one o'clock lost sight of land (the Lizard) in evening – seasickish.' He described to his mother the loading of the ship's stores: 'Fowls, Ducks, Turkeys, all alive and squatted down under legs of beef, hampers and vegetables. One unfortunate Duck got away, and a chase ensued – I should have liked to let him off, but the poor fool did not know how to use his fortune and instead of making for the shore, kept quacking with absurd vehemence close to us.'

Their first sight of a foreign land was of Portugal. The Portuguese coast was 'the first foreign soil I have come near'. About forty miles from land, they were presented with an apocalyptic sight: 'We have just come across a dead horse and a shark at him.'

On Saturday 15 December they were in Cadiz harbour but not allowed to land. They took on passengers and proceeded to Gibraltar which they reached in the early evening. The Sunday was spent in quarantine and the *Hermes* shipped coal. On Monday 18 they were allowed ashore on what Newman described to Harriett as 'the first foreign land I ever set foot on'.

From there they went on to Malta but were not allowed to land because of fears about cholera. Christmas Day was spent in taking on coals and Newman wrote to Harriett that it was 'the most wretched Christmas Day I conceive it to be my lot to suffer'. His meditations on Christ's birthday and on a place where an Apostle had been, prompted him to write, 'Surely there is something very wrong in the actual state of the Church in England – we are neither one thing or the other; neither strong enough to command obedience, nor loose enough to protest in our separate persons.' Experience of other places, and an objectivity brought about by distance, were revealing deficiencies in his Church.

They set sail for Corfu on 26 December, put in to Zante, and reached Patras on 29. He was enchanted by Greece, by its climate, its people, its direct associations with the Classical literature he had known since youth. He admired the picturesque dress of the men which he recalled Byron had spoken of in *Childe Harold*, 'the snowy camese', 'then an embroidered waistcoat – a plaited and frilled white petticoat to the shins and a large great coat with the arms hanging down behind'. These were fine figures, and their coffee 'was almost the best I ever tasted – and so refreshing, I could fancy I had been drinking wine'.

They reached Corfu, where Newman visited some Greek Orthodox Churches and the English garrison. He enjoyed the delicacies, a Turkish sweet made of honey and 'otto of roses', a Corfu one made of almonds and honey, developed a taste for Ithaca wine, 'a great deal of flavours and in no respect heavy', and did not neglect to collect seeds for his mother's garden. On 6 January 1833, they turned back for Patras and eventually reached Malta on 10 January. The next day they were moved into quarantine in the Lazaret and the *Hermes* went on homeward bound. Newman recorded his experiences of the Lazaret for Jemima and described how the place seemed haunted by footsteps, and an evil spirit sitting by Froude's bed. No doubt there were strange sounds, and the boredom of the Lazaret was acute, but Newman was a connoisseur of ghost-stories, and, it should be remembered, entertained his mother and sisters with them. He had no time for quarantine regulations, 'The system of quarantine is the most absurd of all conceivable humbugs, but the British are obliged by other powers to keep it up.' On 23 January they were released, but Newman developed a severe cold which confined his movements and he saw little of Malta. February 7 saw them leaving Malta for Naples: the voyage took them to Messina and Palermo from where Newman travelled by mule to Segesta. 'It has been a day in my life to see Egesta, it is hitherto the flower of our expedition – from the moment I saw Sicily, I kept saying to myself "This is Sicily".' Sicily made such an impression on him that he wanted to savour it often, 'as one smells again and again at a sweet flower'.

In Naples he learned about the Church Temporalities Bill and wrote to his mother just before leaving for Rome, 'We have just heard the Irish Church Reform Bill – well done my blind Premier, confiscate and rob, till, like Samson, you pull down the political structure on your own head, tho' without his deliberate purpose and good cause.' The Bill became law in July 1833, abolishing ten sees of the established Church in Ireland and raised taxes on bishoprics, chapters and rich benefices. Previously revenues for church expenses had been levied on the general population who were, of course, largely Roman Catholic. Newman and like-minded Anglicans saw the measure as interference by the State in Church affairs which had to be immediately condemned.

Rome was a great pleasure. The whole of the voyage so far had encouraged him to write many poems which were sent back home in letters to his mother and sisters: from Rome he sent his first two Sacred poems, Lyra Apostolica, to Hugh Rose for publication in the *British Magazine*. He visited churches, and monuments, admired the Apollo Belvedere and was overcome by Raphael's figures in the Vatican museum. He met Nicholas Wiseman, Rector of the English College in Rome and later Archbishop of Westminster and a cardinal. Rome was, like Oxford, 'calm, quiet, so dignified and beautiful', but he saw no chance of the Roman and the English Churches coming to terms, 'A union with Rome, while it is what it is, is impossible; it is a dream. As to the individual member of the cruel church, who can but love and feel for them?' St Peter's, illuminated, was particularly 'a splendid sight'.

Writing to John Christie, a Fellow of Oriel, on 6 April, Newman showed that he had decided to return to Sicily. The Froudes, not wanting another long sea voyage had decided to return to England by land, while Newman was 'drawn by an irresistible attraction to the fair levels and richly verdured heights of Sicily. What a country it is! a shadow of Eden, so as at once to enrapture and to make one melancholy. It will be a vision for my whole life; and, though I should not choose, I am not sorry to go alone, in order, as Wordsworth would say, to commune with high nature.'

The Froudes having left, Newman stayed behind in Naples, visiting Mount Vesuvius before setting off for Sicily. He described how, on the mountain side, the silence was imposing until an ear was put to some small crevice when 'you hear a rushing sound, deep and hollow, part of wind and part of the internal commotion of the mountain'. He descended

300 feet down into the crater, and because his shoes did not fit properly they became filled with hot ashes: 'I can only say that I found both my hands and the soles of my feet blistered all over on my return home.'

He was forced to wait for a passage to Sicily until 19 April. He passed the time sight-seeing, writing letters, preaching, dining out. He told his mother how well the Neapolitans prepared liver, giblets and spinach, all of which he could not abide in England. He attributed a nightmare to some tempting cheese which he had tried. Part of the nightmare was a tiresome college meeting after which he wanted to retire to some attractive shrubberies to recover himself. He commented later, interestingly enough, that they were those of his father's house at Ham 'and when I dreamed of heaven, as a boy, it was always of Ham.'

Sicily did not turn out as expected. By good fortune, he had taken on a servant named Gennaro, a veteran of the Peninsular War, who had spent sixteen years in the service of an English family. With him he crossed to Messina and together they made for Catania. On 26 April they went by sea on a 'speronara', a thirty-five foot long sailing boat, to Syracuse. There, besides reading Thucydides and visiting places of historical interest, he was entertained by people of the local community. Two days later Newman embarked for the voyage back to Catania but a change of wind forced them to shelter in a cave north of Syracuse. At dawn they went to Augusta and from there he made the journey by mule to Catania, a 'toilsome journey' of thirty-two miles, and on arrival he felt 'more dead than alive'. He rested for a day but on 30 April 'some feverishness' came on him. Determined to see Agrigento and feeling slightly better, he struck out for the middle of the island from where he intended to make for the south coast. Wednesday 1 May was not a day for travel, yet in heavy rain he made his way to Adrano. The next day he reached Leonforte, as his diary records, 'very weak and ill'. He had to stay there until 6 May unable to proceed, and the seriousness of his illness can be judged from the brief note written on the inside cover of his notebook, addressed to Hurrell Froude. Gennaro thought Newman was dying and if this were to be so Froude had to be the one to break the news of his death to his mother. He wrote later that he could not believe that he was really going to die: 'I could not help saying, "I must act as if I were to die, but I think God has work for me yet".' Rashly, he anticipated his recovery too soon, and on 6 May resumed his journey. It was too much for him and about seven miles out of Leonforte he completely broke down. Fortunately a doctor was in the vicinity, tended to him, and finally Newman was moved on to Castro Giovanni where lodging was found. His diary entry for 7 May reads, 'I recollect in these days taking salts, and castor oil (which I thought James's powder).' The 13th of May he reckoned to be the crisis of his illness and after that he gradually began to

18. Newman's manuscript of 'Lead, Kindly Light', the hymn written during his journey in 1833 from Palermo to Marseilles

recover. His journey to Agrigento was given up. He decided to head straight for Palermo, thence to Marseilles. He wrote to Frederic Rogers that he had lost Agrigento and Selinunte, but he 'did not know before nature could be so beautiful. It *is* a country. It passes belief. It is like the garden of Eden.' At least he had seen Taormina.

The *Apologia* tells how he was forced for want of a vessel to spend three weeks at Palermo. At last he secured a passage on an orange boat, bound for Marseilles. During the voyage, the ship was becalmed for a week in the Straits of Bonifacio and it was there that he spent most of his time writing verses. The major composition of this ordeal was *The Pillar of the Cloud* better known by its opening words 'Lead, kindly light.' His illness was at an end and he now felt the need to get back to work with extreme urgency. As he had foreseen, there was much to be done. 'I was aching to get home', he wrote in the *Apologia*.

There is no doubt that Newman saw his illness as a critical stage in his religious development. A year later he wrote a detailed memoir of the experience. Already, on 4 August 1833, he had written to Henry Wilberforce that he felt God was opposing him in his Sicilian illness, and it led him to discover sins in his conduct, 'which had led God thus to fight against me'. He saw that there was a wilfulness about his spirit: it had led him to return to Sicily when perhaps he ought to have gone home. As he lay ill he realized that almost three years before to the day the crisis over his Tutorship had come to a head, and perhaps his manner in dealing with the difference of opinion between himself and Hawkins had been hasty and impatient. Then he remembered his farewell sermon preached the day before he left against Wilfulness. He confided to Wilberforce 'that I seemed to be predicting my own condemnation'. He regretted the strength of his resentment against Hawkins, and yet still felt that God did not utterly condemn him: 'I had not run counter to any advice given me, and I said, "I have not sinned against the light"', and repeated this often. The illness was clearly a crucial moral lesson for him as well as a form of physical punishment.

On 27 June he had reached Marseilles and on the evening of the following day he set off for Lyons, eager to be back in England. Again he over-exerted himself, and tired out had to rest for several days in Lyons. Then he was off again and, apart from an enforced delay in Paris, he did not stop until he was home.

In retrospect, across the distance of years, he saw his illness in Sicily as one of three crises brought about by Divine Providence in his life. Each one, he thought, gave his life new purpose and direction. He wrote in his Journal on 25 June 1869:

Another thought has come on me, that I have had three great illnesses in my life, and how they have turned out! The first keen, terrible one, when I was a boy of fifteen, and it made me a Christian – with experience before and after, awful and known only to God. My second, not painful, but tedious and shattering, was that which I had in 1827, when I was one of the Examining Masters, and it too broke me off from an incipient liberalism, and determined my religious course. The third was in 1833, when I was in Sicily, before the commencement of the Oxford Movement.

Whether or not the illnesses were acts of Providence, the languor of his sickness in Sicily made him all the more earnest to pursue the interests of the Church on his return. The interference in Church affairs, especially by the Whigs in Parliament, had to be opposed. He determined to do this with vigour.

The Vicar of St Mary's arrived at his mother's house at Rose Hill at 7 pm on 9 July, where Frank, by chance, had just arrived from Persia. 'What a joy it is to be back!' he wrote to Keble, 'yet somehow I thought of it far more while I was cramped up in my Italian vessel than now I am arrived – and I cannot quite see the philosophy of this phenomenon – except, I suppose, that our sensations of pain are more vivid than those of pleasure.' The following Sunday Keble preached the Assize sermon in St Mary's on the subject of National Apostasy.

19. John Keble by John Bacon. Newman considered his Assize sermon, preached in Oxford on 14 July 1833, as the beginning of the Oxford Movement

Chapter 4   From Oxford to Rome 1833–45

'The Parting of Friends.'   J. H. Newman

Keble's morning sermon preached before the Judges of Assize in St Mary's Church on Sunday 14 July 1833 has long been marked as the proper beginning of the Oxford Movement. Certainly Newman saw it as such. He wrote in the *Apologia*, 'It was published under the title of "National Apostasy". I have ever considered and kept the day, as the start of the religious movement of 1833.'

For some time Keble had been unhappy about the state both of the Church and the nation. The Hanoverian years had seen the Church in torpor: the convocations were silent, daily services ignored, holy days unobserved, pastoral responsibilities neglected. The effect of this torpor as the decades of the nineteenth century progressed was to erode the authority of the Church. Already there had been the repeal of the Test Act, the Act of Catholic Emancipation, and the Reform Act of 1832. The episcopate was about to be undermined by an Act suppressing ten Irish sees. It was time to speak out. As Keble said, 'Scoundrels must be called scoundrels.' His St Mary's sermon gave the opportunity. Unequivocally Keble denounced the infidels whom he saw, especially in parliament, interfering in Church affairs. He reminded the nation of its responsibilities towards the principles of religion embodied in the Church of England and told off the apostates, those who had turned away from God altogether. He stoutly defended the bishops and complained that 'the disrespect of the successors of the Apostles, as such, is an unquestionable symptom of enmity to Him, who gave them their commission at first, and has pledged Himself to be with them for ever'.

The Irish bishoprics were suppressed in spite of the forebodings expressed by Keble and his friends. The Assize sermon went largely unheeded. The depredators of the Church of England were at large, and busily at work. Keble decided to publish his sermon which Newman enthusiastically applauded, and it helped to encourage a great deal of activity among churchmen and mobilized them into defending the Church. Newman's 'fragmentary diary' for the latter half of 1833 described how people met, talked and wrote to others in the cause of Church defence. Tracts were begun, suggestions put forward about organization. Already moves had been made. Writing to Henry Wilberforce on 16th July, Newman had informed him, 'We have set up societies here – for the defence of the liturgy and the enforcement of the doctrine of the Apostolical Succession. They are already forming in Oxfordshire, Berkshire, Gloucestershire, Devonshire, Kent and Essex and Suffolk.' Clearly these societies were gentlemanly affairs and not political machines: Keble had a strong aversion to 'parties'. Later in the year Newman recorded that his views on procedure had crystallized, 'I was strongly against an Association, (i.e. any body in which a majority bound a minority,) and liked Keble's way of putting it – "We pledge ourselves one to another in our several stations, reserving our Canonical obedience".' A strong division of opinion gradually developed between those who favoured an association and those who did not. The latter decided that a series of tracts should be written and circulated. These would concentrate on the basic principles of the Church and reassert apostolical and therefore episcopal authority. It was felt that any firmly established society or association would challenge episcopal authority.

Feelings about 'The Church Temporalities (Ireland) Bill' were certainly running high and many influential and intelligent men in the Church of England, besides Newman and Keble, were pricked into action. Newman's old confederate, the editor of the *British Magazine*, the man to whom Newman sent many of his Lyra Apostolica for publication in the journal, called an important meeting of like-minded thinkers at his Hadleigh rectory. Newman told Charles Golightly, an Oriel friend, of the meeting, 'Rose of Cambridge is now holding a conference at his living in Essex [Suffolk] of men similarly minded – our deputies to it are Froude and Palmer. They are talking over the most important ecclesiastical questions – Percival is there, and Lyall and others.' This was about as far as combination went.

The movement to produce tracts gained the upper hand and the preference of the strategists, although at the same time Newman felt it not improper to form what he called 'Friends of the Church' in order to encourage the clergy to stand firm on the doctrine of the apostolical succession and to defend the integrity of the liturgy. The Friends were to be based in Oxford. On the day that he explained this to Froude, 9 September 1833, the first of the *Tracts for the Times*, an appeal to the clergy was published. Isaac Williams wrote that he liked it very much and was just sorry that Newman's name did not appear as its author. Newman busily asked others to write for the series.

Keble's sermon had quickly proved to be the rallying call to the defenders of the faith. At the same time as this campaign was being launched in the Church's defence, Newman was busy on other affairs. On 16 September he sent four sketches of history from the Early Church Fathers to Rose for publication in the *British Magazine* and informed him

that he could call on him for as many more as he liked. On 17 October
Oriel held its annual election of college officers. Newman was made Dean
and immediately began his year of office that Michaelmas term. Four days
later he began writing a series of letters to the editor of the *Record* about
church reform, advocating a revival of church discipline and a duty to
follow unflinchingly 'the law and the testimony'. Interference with the
form of services, such as the Commination service or the service for the
Burial of the Dead, was roundly condemned. Then, at the end of October,
there was sad news. Froude, for the sake of his health, decided to leave
Oxford for good, and the next month he set sail for Barbados where he
hoped the climate would preserve his life. Newman lost, with his departure, his greatest friend, confidant and lieutenant.

   At about this time there is the first mention of a petition to the Archbishop of Canterbury. Newman wrote to Samuel Rickards on 29 October
that many influential people were lending support to such an idea: 'We
talk of an Address to the Archbishop declaratory of our attachment to the
Doctrine and Discipline of the Church.' Much of the rest of that year was
spent rallying signatories for the address.

   In the meantime, and at last, Newman's *Arians of the Fourth Century* was
published. His diary records, 'My book out *The Arians* – gave it to Palmer,
Provost, Pusey, Archdeacon Froude,' and several others.

   By 22 November Newman was able to report to Rickards, 'The Address
goes on splendidly – already I believe we have 2000 Clergy who will sign
it.' On 15 December, writing to Froude, Newman commented, with
regard to both the address and the *Tracts*, 'Everything is going on nicely.'
Affairs in college were relatively calm, too: 'I have got thro' the Term
without any kind of rumpus with the Provost and was boasting to Keble.
Alas! this morning I have had a slight difference about shutting up
Chapel.'

   In the new year 1834, he continued writing for Rose the Church of the
Fathers series and the Lyra. The first rumblings were heard of the
controversy over the Moral Philosophy Professorship. Newman wondered about himself as a possible candidate for the chair, and Henry
Woodgate, a one-time Fellow of St John's and friend of Newman's, told
him, 'Act on your own judgement . . . If you can get appointed, pray do so.'
He confided to Bowden that he thought he had a chance of being elected,
but protested that he had 'no special wish for it'. It would have meant a
line of reading different from his then present course.

   His dearest and closest friends were firm supporters of his cause.
Bowden, amongst many others, offered his support after enquiring, 'Is the
chair of Moral Philosophy an object to you?' Later in his life, commenting
on his correspondence and on this letter of Bowden's in particular, New-

man made an historically interesting and characteristically witty aside on nineteenth-century letter-writing. Bowden wrote that he was emphatically grateful for a letter from Newman which he had just received. Newman noted, 'Before the penny post letters were few, and long – which I think will explain my silence. One did not write without a good deal to say, and (a second obstacle) saying a good deal.'

Before the professorship was decided, the address to the Archbishop of Canterbury was prepared for presentation. Deputies from all over the country simulating a lower House of Convocation were to meet at Rivington's, the publishers, and thence to proceed to Lambeth Palace. Keble was among the presenters. Newman informed Henry Wilberforce, 'Keble is one of the Oxford delegates to the Archbishop – at first only official persons were taken – but dear Pusey falling ill, Keble has been selected as being (like Aristides) the nearest approach to an official person of any not in office.' On the 6 February it was handed in, and a few days later Newman wrote to Bowden that 6,500 names were on it but there were more to come in, from the Bishops of Exeter and Llandaff and from other places. In the end, 7,000 signatories supported it.

The Moral Philosophy Professorship was decided on 7 March and the decision went against him. Hawkins had again managed to fix matters in favour of the Principal of St Mary Hall, Renn Dickson Hampden, and Routh, the President of Magdalen, a keen supporter of Newman and his principles, was extremely upset. Even so Hampden was a considerable opponent, a Head of House, Bampton Lecturer, an Aristotelian, and a Liberal. Four days later Newman passed on the news to Wilberforce, 'I give you without delay intelligence of an important event, viz my having been floored as regards the Professorship.' In Greek he noted from Aeschylus, 'I have met my conqueror and departed.' Hampden, who had taken over Newman's pupils when he ceased to be Tutor of Oriel, had triumphed.

Although disappointed, at the same time he was cheered by the impact which the Tracts were making. He was delighted by attacks printed in the *Christian Observer*, and some Birmingham reformer had denounced Newman as the editor of the Tracts. He remarked happily to Wilberforce, 'Surely there is something very powerful and irritating in our view, when it can raise wrath in sets of men so differing from each other – a potent rhetoric truly, which affects such different hearers.' Such interest and virulent reaction could only mean that the *Tracts* were being read: men's minds were being stirred.

Whereas the *Tracts* made what might be called a popular and general attack on the minds and consciences of Anglican clergy and congregations alike, Newman's sermons provided the spiritual and intellectual suste-

nance which lay behind that assault. In March 1834 he published his first
volume of *Parochial and Plain Sermons*, after which he maintained a steady
run of publications of this sort. It was the custom for Anglican preachers
to read their sermons which meant that usually they were carefully
written and so easy to prepare for publication. Denied a professorial chair
from which to lecture, Newman found his own platform in the Adam de
Brome Chapel in St Mary's. He wrote in his diary for 25 June, 'Lecture in
evening in Adam de Br's chapel on public prayers – stated intention of
beginning daily service.' Earlier he had explained to Froude that he
thought he would do as Keble did and institute a reading of daily service
in his church. He wrote that he would announce his intention 'of reading
the Morning Service daily in the Chancel while and whenever I am in
Oxford – according to the injunctions of the Church – whether people
attend or not'. Although it was not a popular service with the majority of
his congregation, his celebration of the Holy Communion each Sunday
was, and as in many other aspects of church services Newman and the
Oxford Movement were responsible for reviving and establishing the
pattern of services which takes place in the parish churches today.

At this time in the thirties Oxford was fast becoming liberal not only in
political opinions, but also in religious principles. Some would say that it
had long before become liberal in religious matters: indeed, liberal was the
wrong word, for like much of the country it had become lax. The Oxford
Movement reasserted ancient principles and revived neglected practices,
and held to what it saw as the traditional and tried structures of the
Church. This clearly meant that Newman was against liberal interpretation of doctrine or behaviour. He caused a minor furore in pursuing his
duties as Vicar of St Mary's. He was called upon to marry a woman who,
he discovered, was not baptized. He recorded in his diary for 1 July:
'declined to marry Miss Jubber as being unbaptized. (a row followed)',
and in addition wrote a memorandum on the affair recalling his conversation with her father:

> Has she been Baptized?
> No.
> Indeed! (in a lower tone of voice) really, I cannot marry her.
> Well, that *is* superstition – that is superstition indeed.
> Why, how can I, (give Christian marriage), to one who is still an outcast?
> That *is* superstition.
> Mr. Jubber, I did not come here that you might teach me, but to tell you my
>   feelings of duty.
> Sir, I do not wish you of course to act against your sense of duty – There are
>   several clergymen quite desirous to marrying them.

By the following Saturday, the affair was in the newspapers. He was sent the following extract from the *Weekly Dispatch* of 6 July, by a correspondent in Richmond:

The Vicar of St Mary the Virgin parish Oxford, in his hyper-anxiety to signalize his zeal against dissent and in favour of 'orthodoxy' refused on Tuesday last to marry a young couple of very respectable connexions in that City solely because the blooming to be Bride had not been christened, and was in the rev: bigot's phraseology an *outcast*, the matrimonial knot was however tied directly afterwards by the more tolerant and less pharisaical minister of a neighbouring parish-church, and the happy pair were very properly relieved from the cruel disappointment which threatened them.

The line was being drawn by Newman: others supported him. Isaac Williams, another contributor to the *Tracts*, stated that people should be told whether or not they were heathens. Keble and Pusey both wrote to Newman in support. Pusey said, 'I am glad of what you have done, and trust it will do good "thro' evil report and good report".' As Pusey predicted the story got into most of the papers, even *The Times* where Bowden read about it. Mr Jubber wrote a letter to the Oxford paper, to which Newman replied in all charity. The business fizzled out with the Bishop of Oxford agreeing that Newman should in future say that he was marrying unbaptized people at the Bishop's direction.

A stand on principle had been made and although the *Weekly Dispatch* was not right about motivation, Newman's alleged 'zeal against dissent', it is understandable why the reporter should have thought it so. Liberal forces in Oxford were working keenly for the admission of dissenters to the University. Naturally, Newman was opposed to this measure and campaigned vigorously against it, as he did against any interference with the marriage laws. He had been active in rallying members of the University to sign an Oxford Declaration against the Admission of Dissenters which had been got up in May of 1834. The declaration put forward the view that Oxford was an Anglican foundation and that it was necessary to subscribe to the Thirty-Nine Articles of Faith of the Church of England, in order to be a member and proceed to a degree, and that it was the duty of those such as Newman to continue their present system of religious instruction. It appeared that conservative opinion in the University prevailed, and in Parliament too, for the Bill to admit Dissenters to the Universities was defeated in the Lords at the beginning of August.

Hampden, however, suddenly changed sides and towards the end of August published 'Observations on Religious Dissent with particular reference to the use of religious tests in the University'. Newman wrote to Rose, 'Hampden, Principal of St Mary Hall, has just published a pamphlet which, I fear, destroys our glory. Hitherto Oxford was all on one side, as far as print goes, in this late dispute with the Commons and Co.'

A move to admit dissenters to the University was made again in March 1835 when the Earl of Radnor re-opened the question of subscription to the Thirty-Nine Articles in Parliament. Oxford brought the matter before Convocation which met in the Sheldonian Theatre on 20 May. Hurrell Froude, who had been allowed to return to England by his father as summer approached, journeyed to Oxford for the vote. The proposal before the House of Convocation was that instead of compulsory subscription to the Thirty-Nine Articles by members of the University, there should simply be introduced an innovation, a Declaration of Conformity to the Church of England. The motion was heavily defeated by 459 to 57. Newman wrote in his diary, 'In our College 38 non-residents came up – of whom 37 were with us – the one being not a clear non-resident but a fellow. Large dinner in hall'. The liberals were once again put down. Hurrell Froude had cast his last vote. On 4 June he went down to Devonshire and was never to see Oxford again.

In February of the following year, 1836 he died, aged thirty-three. The dreaded disease of nineteenth-century England, consumption, had claimed him. Archdeacon Froude wrote to Newman on 28 February 'My son died this day ... About two o'clock as I was recommending him to take some egg and wine, I observed a sudden difficulty in his breathing and some weak efforts to free his throat from accumulated mucus. He attempted to speak, and then after a few slight struggles his sufferings were at an end.' Newman was grief-stricken: he opened the archdeacon's sad letter in Tom Mozley's room and was unable to utter a word. A day later he wrote to Bowden:

He was so very dear to me, that it is an effort to me to reflect on my own thoughts about him. I can never have a greater loss, looking on for the whole of life – for he was to me, and he was likely to be ever, in the same degree of continual familiarity which I enjoyed with yourself in our Undergraduate days ... yet it has pleased God to take him, in mercy to him, but by a very heavy visitation to all who were intimate with him. Yet everything was so bright and beautiful about him, that to think of him must always be a comfort. The sad feeling I have is, that one cannot retain on one's memory, all one wishes to keep there and that as year passes after year, the image of him will be fainter and fainter.

On 20 March he informed Maria Giberne, a close friend of the family, of Froude's death, and confided, 'I love to think and muse upon one who had the most angelic mind of any person I ever fell in with ... You will do me a most exceeding kindness in giving me your sketch of him.' To Keble and to Newman himself, two of Hurrell Froude's 'Fratres desideratissimi', fell the task of editing his literary remains.

So far as Lord Radnor's Bill was concerned, it made progress until 14 July 1835 when it was rejected by the House of Lords. The line had held against the liberals. As in sign of celebration, a week later the first stone of Littlemore's own church was able to be laid by Mrs Newman; and towards the end of the year Pusey committed himself to the Movement.

Early in 1836 Hampden was enjoying considerable influence, when it happened that the Regius Professor of Divinity, Edward Burton, a Canon of Christ Church and Rector of Ewelme fell ill. Newman's fears were mentioned in a letter written in parts over several days to Froude: 'We are very anxious today at the news of Burton's serious indisposition – inflammation of the chest. It would be a blow indeed if the Whigs were to appoint a Professor. Arnold, I suppose, would be the man. Jan 22. Burton, as you know is gone. Milman has a chance? yet I think the Ministers will not run their heads against a wall.' Keble was rumoured to be a possibility for the chair: Newman had it from Rose. In the end, though, prospects were dreary for the Movement's supporters. Newman conveyed his pessimism to Keble and thought that the chances of their friends were very slight.

Newman's diary entry for 8 February reads tersely, 'News of Hampden's appointment in Burton's place,' but the same day he wrote to Rose, 'Pusey wishes me to tell you that we have begun a petition to the King against the appointment of Hampden, begging him to give the Archbishop a veto.' Two days later Keble showed what was felt by the rest of the Tractarians, or the Puseyites as they were now coming to be called: 'What can be done? I should think a sort of respectful memorial to the Archbishops and Bishops might be got up, stating *facts* merely, as to what Hampden has taught and as to what influence he would have, and leaving them to judge whether something should not be done to remove candidates for Orders out of his reach'; and on that day Newman began his pamphlet against Hampden which when published on 13 February was called *Elucidations of Dr Hampden's theological statements*. It ran to forty-seven pages under nine heads: doctrinal truths, the Trinity, the Incarnation, the Atonement, the Sacraments, original sin, the soul, morals, positive statements.

Although Newman's *Elucidations* opened the eyes of many to the meaning of the Movement, and brought some new blood to the cause, Hampden was no mean opponent. When the Heads of the Oxford colleges met to consider his appointment and consider voting their disapproval, Hampden himself turned up as was his right. Newman told Bowden that the Dean of Christ Church asked Hampden if he meant to remain: 'We are going to talk about you,' and that the Professor answered in the affirmative. Newman went on, 'Shuttleworth asked him if he meant to vote? he said he should be guided by circumstances – Gilbert and Symons conducted the attack. Hampden turned to the Vice-Chancellor "as head of the present inquisition" and told him he would find as bad things in the sermons of Mr Pusey, Newman or Hook. He ended up by voting for himself and just turning the scale thereby.'

It was generally thought that Hampden's elevation was effected by the lobbying of Whately, and that Thomas Arnold had declined the chair before Hampden had accepted it. No Movement candidate stood a chance of appointment, and a little earlier in the month Bowden had advised caution on the general front. He wrote, 'I am rather anxious . . . that your anti-popery Tracts should be soon out. If but one apostolical should unfortunately fall into that system, it would be a fearful blow to us all.' In retrospect, those words are charged with irony because of Newman's own conversion to Rome, but they did at the time prompt him to start preparing a justification of the Movement's middle way for the Church of England.

Poor Hampden was to go on suffering attack for many months. Late in March proceedings were launched against him in Convocation, but the Oxford proctors vetoed them. Immediately, members, prominent among them Pusey and Newman, drew up a new requisition to the Vice-Chancellor to start proceedings which would clear the University from the charge of sanctioning such principles as Hampden taught. Finally on 5 May they were successful. The 'Statute' against Hampden was carried in Convocation by 474 votes to 94: again the country clergy had been called on: the 'men had been called up'.

Hampden's persecution continued even after Newman had left the Church of England. In 1847 when Lord John Russell became Prime Minister he chose Hampden, at the earliest opportunity, as Bishop of Hereford. Once more Puseyites, with Keble leading them, tried their strength against the State: they went in deputation to the Bishop of Oxford, Samuel Wilberforce. Wilberforce, not having a bishop's palace in Oxford, stayed with Provost Hawkins at Oriel who according to Frank Newman made the Bishop read Hampden's work for the first time over-night before meeting Keble. His reported response to Keble's complaint was 'I have now read Hampden myself, and cannot presume to blame him.' On this occasion the Puseyite attack foundered.

The rest of the year 1836 was as busy as usual for Newman. In April his sister Jemima married John Mozley whose father was a prominent printer in Derby. Three weeks later Mrs Newman died at the age of sixty-three. This was another grievous blow for Newman coming so soon after Hurrell Froude's death, and it affected him deeply. He informed his Aunt Elizabeth of what had happened:

My dearest Mother is taken from us. If you knew how dreadfully she has suffered in mind, and how little her wanderings left her like herself, you would feel, as we

20. The interior of Littlemore Church, 1839, from a painting
by J. Buckler. A chancel and a tower were added in 1848

do, that it really is a release. Who would have thought it! Every thing is strange in
this world – every thing mysterious. Nothing but sure faith can bring us through.
My dear Mother was not herself even before the end – she sank into a slumber and
so died. She seemed so strong and well, it is most surprising. Little did I think,
when she laid the first stone at the new Church, she would not live to see it
finished.

A memorial tablet was put up to her in the church at Littlemore and her
corpse buried in St Mary's. Harriett, bearing up under the strain and now
left on her own, visited her sister and the Mozleys at Derby and towards
the end of September she married Thomas who was later to write *Reminiscences of Oriel College and the Oxford Movement* which Newman criticized
severely for inaccuracy.

Away from the domestic front, there was much work to be done in
writing and organizing tracts, lobbying against Hampden, preaching,
lecturing, and in September planning with Pusey the *Library of the Fathers*.

He supervised, too, the building of Littlemore Church which was consecrated on the 22nd of that month. Richard Bagot, Bishop of Oxford, liked
Newman's sermon so much that he asked him for a copy. Newman was
also sustaining attacks on himself for what were called 'Romanist' tendencies. In April Bowden had asked for assurance that Dr Nicholas Wiseman,
who was Rector of the English College in Rome, had not been in Oxford as
Newman's guest; he wanted an answer which would prevent his good
name being spoken evil of. Newman replied, 'The simple answer is, that,
to the best of my belief, Dr Wiseman has not been in Oxford, at least not in
the University, though he may have passed through in a coach.' He went
on to say that of course had Wiseman come to Oxford, he would have
returned the civility which Wiseman had shown Newman when he was
visiting Rome.

At the end of the year Newman found himself accused by a correspondent called Henin. He wrote of Newman that his 'views on the Priesthood
and Sacraments are such as the Romanists adopt is what *many* believe',
and went on that his 'views are effecting a fearful deviation from the faith
once delivered to the Saints and if not at present popery, will ere long lead
to that awful apostasy.' Some days later, Samuel Wood, an old Oriel man
and a barrister, wrote that one or two people were upset by Newman's
Wiseman article in the *British Magazine*: 'They say you make Wiseman a
peg to hang your attacks on Protestantism on.'

The combined effect of Hampden, and the increasing conviction of
many Church of England clergy and laymen, that Newman and his
Tractarians were trailing their coats too obviously and energetically for
Romanism, led him to prepare a series of works in defence of Anglo-
Catholicism. In the *Apologia* Newman pays tribute to the effect of Pusey on
the Movement: 'Without him we should have had no chance, especially at
the early date of 1834, of making any serious resistance to the liberal
aggression.' His personal qualities were of even greater significance: 'He
saw that there ought to be more sobriety, more gravity, more careful
pains, more sense of responsibility in the Tracts and in the whole Movement.' There is no doubt that Pusey's influence, as well, urged Newman to
defend the Anglo-Catholic position in print. The first of his series was
published in March 1837 and had been in preparation since 1834. It was
entitled *The Prophetical Office of the Church viewed relatively to Romanism and
Popular Protestantism*, and was a justification for the Via Media, a receding
from extremes. In his introduction he conceded that 'Protestantism and
Popery are real religions ... but the Via Media, viewed as an integral
system, has scarcely had existence except on paper'. He accepted both the
objection and the task to lessen it, and he proceeded to talk about
Anglo-Catholicism as 'the religion of Andrewes, Laud, Hammond, Butler

and Wilson', one which had to be as real as 'Romanism or popular Protestantism'. It was his and the Tractarians' duty to clarify it as such, and not regard it as a 'modification or transition-state' of either. *The Prophetical Office* was followed in March 1838 by his volume on *Justification*, in May on the *Disquisition on the Canon of Scripture* and in June on the *Tractate on Anti Christ*. The contents of these four books were originally worked out for, and delivered as, lectures in the Adam de Brome Chapel of St Mary's and they did much to form a school of opinion which 'grew stronger and stronger every year, till it came into collision with the nation, and with the church of the nation, which it began by professing especially to serve.'

At the same time, in 1838, he became editor of the *British Critic* which was naturally for the three years of his rule the chief organ of the Movement; but the first signs of real crisis showed themselves as well. Bishop Bagot in a Charge made some 'light animadversions' on the *Tracts for the Times*. Newman offered immediately, in deference to his bishop's authority, to stop the *Tracts*. On this occasion Bagot declined to press the point.

The year 1839 occupied Newman with his usual crowded, busy routine of domestic, pastoral and scholarly duties. In the end it proved to be the crucial year for him in which his mind was turned distinctly away from the Church of England and what he called its 'Via Media.' He began to succumb to two attacks made on him by the Church of Rome, the first made inadvertently. He called it 'the first hit from Rome'; and it was in Shakespeare's words 'a palpable hit'.

He had begun a scholarly, theological study of the doctrine of the Incarnation and the controversy that arose in the fifth century over the single or dual nature of Christ. The Council of Chalcedon determined Roman Catholic and Greek Orthodox doctrine on the nature of Christ. The Catholic Church pronounced Christ indivisible, in two natures God and Man; the Greek Orthodox Church pronounced Christ of two natures. The two small words 'in' or 'of' meant a world of differences. Large sectors of the Church could not accept the idea of two natures in Christ which, as it were, had not coalesced. So the Monophysite heresy grew up whose adherents upheld the single, coalesced nature of Christ. The Church of England expresses the Catholic position in the Second of the Thirty-nine Articles, 'Two whole and perfect Natures, that is to say, the Godhead and Manhood, were joined together in one Person, never to be divided, whereof is one Christ, very God, and very Man'.

Having finished his reading of this period of Church history, he paused and reflected. History rather than theology struck him a blow. He saw in the Monophysite position a reflection of his own position and that of his 'Via Media' in relation to the Roman Catholic Church. He wrote, 'I saw my face in that mirror and I was a Monophysite', and continued, 'There was an awful similitude, more awful because so silent and unimpassioned, between the dead records of the past and the feverish chronicle of the present.' He came to think that if in principle the Monophysites were heretical and in schism then so was he. The Church of Rome had remained unwavering: it was the same in the fifth century as it was in the nineteenth. His confidence was more than shaken: it was undermined by history.

The second and equal blow was struck by Nicholas Wiseman, this time by publication in the *Dublin Review*. Wiseman wrote an article in which he compared the Church of England to the Donatists, a schismatic movement which seceded from Rome in the fourth century. Although unlike the Monophysites, the Donatists had not taken a 'middle way' in their actions, Newman nevertheless began to see their error in relation to Rome. Wiseman quoted St Augustine's powerful phrase 'securus judicat orbis terrarum' – 'the whole world is a safe judge' or 'the judgement of the whole world cannot be shaken'. Newman saw his appeal to antiquity demolished. The Church of England, like the Donatists, was condemned. The 'Via Media' weakened by his study of the fifth-century Councils, was well-nigh destroyed by his reading about the Donatists. Wiseman's thrust seemed to have found its mark.

Newman did not admit the effect of the two 'hits', and staunch for that moment at least to the Church of England, he decided that Wiseman should be answered: otherwise what number of people might defect to Rome.

He decided to investigate what could be said 'after all for the Anglican Church, in spite of its acknowledged short-comings.' This task he performed in an article published in the *British Critic* of January 1840. He also saw that whatever men had done to change and modify 'the old Catholic Truth', it still lived on in the Thirty-Nine Articles. His determination was to show how far the Articles of the Church of England could be reconciled to the Roman Catholic Church. The result was *Tract 90*.

All this was in his mind when he retired to Littlemore for the Lent of 1840, a period spent in disciplined life and fasting: 'During the Hebdomada Passions I abstained from milk also, breakfasting on bread and water, except when I took nothing, i.e. Wednesday & Friday.'

Tract 90 was published in 1841: 'The main thesis of the essay was this: the Articles do not oppose catholic teaching; they but partially oppose Roman dogma; they, for the most part, oppose the dominant errors of Rome.' Reaction to the tract was immediate and severe. Oxford took the lead in condemning it. Archibald Tait, then Senior Tutor of Balliol, together with three other senior tutors, wrote an open letter which argued that the *Tracts*, and this one in particular, suggested and opened 'a way by which men might, at least in the case of Roman views, violate their solemn engagements to the University'. The Heads of the Colleges came to the same conclusion and similarly condemned the *Tracts*. Oxford having led the way, the country at large followed in the act of stringent criticism.

For a year he had been considering giving up the editorship of the *British Critic*: in July he decided to resign and handed over to his brother-in-law Thomas Mozley. The Tractarians were under fire from all quarters: confidence was lost and Newman's place as leader was lost. Newman saw this himself and knew deep within his heart his own lack of confidence: 'The one question was, What was I to do? I determined to be guided not by my imagination, but by my reason. Had it not been for this severe resolve, I should have been a catholic sooner than I was.'

His conscience was in turmoil, and later in 1841 he suffered what he described as 'three further blows which broke me'. Looking again at the Arian controversy, he saw in it a parallel to the Monophysite one. He came to see clearly in that period of history, that 'the pure Arians were the Protestants, the semi-Arians were the Anglicans, and that Rome now was what it was then'. His doubts in Anglican catholicity reinforced by this view, he found that the bishops of the Church of England were one by one charging against him and *Tract 90*: it was the only means of direct condemnation in their power. Bishop Bagot saw the trouble and confusion the tract was causing. At first he was conciliatory, but in May 1842 he condemned it. *Tract 90* was the last of the tracts: Newman bowed to the bishops' views and stopped their publication. The third blow came over the Jerusalem Bishopric. Baron von Bunsen, the Prussian diplomat and European Protestant leader whom Newman had sought out in Rome, proposed a joint bishopric there between the Anglican Church and the Prussian Protestant Church. Newman's view was that the Church of England was 'courting an intercommunion with protestant Prussia and the heresy of Orientals, while it forbade any sympathy or concurrence with the church of Rome'. He wrote out a solemn protest and sent it to both the Archbishop of Canterbury and Bagot.

Part VI of the *Apologia* begins, 'From the end of 1841, I was on my death-bed, as regards my membership with the Anglican Church, though at the time I became aware of it only by degrees.' In 1842, following his decision, and his promise to Bagot, not to take part publicly in Church affairs, apart from carrying out his duties at St Mary's, he retired from Oxford to Littlemore. He had bought for himself a small block of L-shaped cottages and stables, which he had converted into the sparsest of living-quarters. These were ready in the spring of 1842, and it was there that he embarked on his study of Athanasius, and began to attract a

21. The 'College', Littlemore. Newman leased this row of cottages from 1842 to 1845. He was received into the Roman Catholic Church here on 9 October 1845. 'In the cells nothing to be seen but poverty and simplicity – bare walls, floor composed of a few rough bricks without a carpet, a straw bed, one or two chairs, and a few books; this comprises the whole furniture! The refectory and kitchen are in the same style, all very small and very poor ... A Capuchin monastery would appear a great place when compared with Littlemore.' – Father Dominic Barberi

number of young men around him, sympathizers who liked the cloistered life.

He was accused of setting up a monastery and locally it became known as the Littlemore Monastery, but he went to great pains to rebut the charge of reviving monastic orders in the Church of England. A newspaper article had asserted that a 'so-called Anglo-Catholic Monastery is in process of erection at Littlemore, and that the cells of dormitories, the chapel, the refectory, the cloisters all may be seen advancing to perfection, under the eye of a Parish Priest of the Diocese of Oxford'. Newman protested to Bagot, 'There is no "chapel"; no "refectory", hardly a dining-room or parlour. The "cloisters" are my shed connecting the cottages. I do not understand what "cells of dormitories" means.'

Scandal-mongers, took no notice, or did not understand. They said that Newman and the young men who were with him at Littlemore were already Roman Catholics. John Dalgairns, whose family were from Guernsey and who could not be elected to a Fellowship of his Oxford College because of his Catholic views, was the first to attach himself to Newman at Littlemore. That year two more joined him, William Lockhart, a connection of Sir Walter Scott's, and Frederick Bowles from neighbouring Abingdon. In 1843 Ambrose St John, Henry Wilberforce's favourite curate, opted for Littlemore. Wilberforce was sad to see him go and warned him against 'shovel-hatted humbug', but nevertheless named his newly-born son Ambrose Newman after his two friends. St John was twenty-eight, mature in character, a keen gardener, and practical. At Christ Church he had worked under Pusey, studying Hebrew and Syriac.

These new friends, whom, he told Jemima, he was most thankful for, were not as old as, nor as brilliant as, his former ones. They did not come to him of his choosing: they came of their own volition. Their friendship was a great consolation in this spiritually troubled time for Newman.

His regimen was demanding. A note of his time-table dated 1842 shows his daily routine. The twenty-four hours were divided as follows: Devotions $4\frac{1}{2}$ hours, study 9 hours, meals 1, recreation $2\frac{3}{4}$, sleep $6\frac{3}{4}$. No talking took place except between two o'clock and half past seven. The day began with him getting up just before five o'clock, and retiring at a quarter past ten.

In the next year Newman took two significant and dramatic steps. He had gradually come to see, as he wrote himself, 'that the Anglican Church was formally in the wrong; on the other (hand), that the church of Rome was formally in the right; then that no valid reason could be assigned for continuing in the Anglican, and again that no valid objections could be taken to joining the Roman.' Firstly, in February he published in the *Conservative Journal* under the heading 'Oxford and Rome' an anonymous 'Retraction of Anti-Catholic Statements'. There was no doubt in anybody's mind that the author was Newman. He explained to his sister that he was merely negating any abuse which he might have levelled at Rome: he was not pronouncing at all on doctrines. He was, it is obvious, clearing his conscience. Secondly, he decided to take a step which he had been considering for three years: he resigned the living of St Mary's. Lockhart had been to hear Luigi Gentili, the Rosminian Order leader, near Loughborough: at that meeting Gentili received him into the Roman Catholic Church. Then, just as Newman was about to write to the Bishop of Oxford, Tom Mozley wrote excitedly to say that he himself was considering conversion to the Roman Church. Newman went to see him and in confidence discussed his own doubts with him. In the end Tom Mozley did not go over, but he resigned his living and took a secular post writing leaders for *The Times*. These incidents reinforced Newman's conviction that his position was untenable. The letter to Bagot was sent. Newman preached his last sermon at St Mary's on 25 September. On the Monday he preached his farewell sermon called 'The Parting of Friends' at Littlemore. A few days later he celebrated the Holy Communion at St Mary's with Pusey which was his last act in the Anglican ministry. Liddon, Pusey's biographer, wrote, 'Some who were in the gloom of that early October morning felt that they were assisting at a funeral of a religious effort which had failed.'

Manning, then Archdeacon of Chichester, wrote asking why he had

22. Newman in 1845, a miniature by Sir William Ross. 'Such *was* our guide, but he has left us to seek our own path: our champion has deserted us – our watchman, whose cry used to cheer us, is heard no more.' – Anne Mozley

resigned. The answer was 'because I think the Church of Rome the Catholic Church, and ours not a part of the Catholic Church, because not in communion with Rome, and I felt I could not honestly be a teacher in it any longer'. To another friend he wrote that this conviction was 'a very different thing from having any intention of joining the church of Rome'. This was to deny the inevitable, and although the progress was slow, it was sure.

At the beginning of 1845, he started to write his *Essay on the Development of Christian Doctrine*. As he worked steadily at it his reservations about the Roman Church gradually disappeared. He wrote in the *Apologia*, 'As I advanced my view so cleared that instead of speaking any more of "the Roman Catholics," I boldly called them Catholics. Before I got to the end, I resolved to be received.'

Newman's move was foreseen by those who knew him. Pusey realized he would go over: Keble waited expectantly and disappointedly: in London Gladstone, kept informed by Manning, calculated the consequences for the established Church. On the Roman Catholic side, Wiseman, now coadjutor to Bishop Walsh in the Midland District and president of Oscott College, waited in prayer and patience. Finally first moves were made: Ambrose St John and Dalgairns, two of his most familiar disciples, went over. Then began the conversion of others in different parts of the country. The way was at last prepared.

On 3 October Newman wrote to the Provost of Oriel resigning his Fellowship. True to character, Newman's old controversialist, Hawkins, replied accepting his resignation but earnestly hoping that Newman would 'still at least be saved from some of the worst errors of the Church of Rome, such as praying to human Mediators or falling down before images'. To the very end Newman's progress was to be made difficult: his unhappy mind and troubled soul was not to receive comfort from any University quarter.

Yet he was resolute: the *Essay on the Development of Christian Doctrine*, whose composition had carried him rationally through the last stages towards Rome, was left unfinished, mid-sentence. Dalgairns had asked Father Dominic Barberi of the Passionist Congregation, who was passing through Oxford, to visit Littlemore. On 8 October Newman wrote to his numerous friends telling them what was about to happen. The letter to Richard Church, who was one of the Oxford proctors to veto the proposal of censure against *Tract 90* and was later to become Dean of St Paul's, began: 'Charissime, I am this night expecting Father Dominic the Passionist.' Another to F. W. Faber said, 'I am this night expecting Father Dominic the Passionist, whom I shall ask to admit me into the One True Fold. This letter will not go till it is over.' Barberi had visited Littlemore

23. Father Dominic Barberi, who
received Newman into the Roman
Catholic Church in 1845

on one occasion before when Newman had met him and been impressed
by his holiness. Dalgairns has recorded that as he left to meet Father
Dominic, Newman quietly said to him, 'When you see your friend, will
you tell him that I wish him to receive me into the Church of Christ?'
When Dalgairns and Father Dominic arrived back in a storm of pouring
rain, Father Dominic placed himself in front of a fire to dry himself: he
described for his superiors what happened next: 'The door opened – and
what a spectacle it was for me to see at my feet John Henry Newman
begging me to hear his confession and admit him into the bosom of the
Catholic Church! And there by the fire he began his general confession
with extraordinary humility and devotion.'

The next morning Father Dominic went into Oxford to the Catholic
Church in St Clement's and informed the priest there of what had
happened. Returning to Littlemore he heard the rest of Newman's confession, and those of Bowles and Richard Stanton who had joined the
disciples that summer.

As the news spread abroad, conversions followed: what had been at first
one or two individuals, became an important number of families, and
professional men. Gladstone's worst fears were realized. The newspapers
proclaimed the establishment's fury.

Chapter 5   Priest and Oratorian 1845–54

'A child of St Philip, my master and guide,
I will live as he lived, and die as he died.'   J. H. Newman

Newman's accession to the Church of Rome brought about consequences which are difficult to evaluate precisely. There is no doubt that the immediate effect on the Church of England was serious. Gladstone was under no illusion at the time and said that Newman's conversion 'has never yet been estimated at anything like the full amount of its calamitous importance'. Numerous waverers followed Newman across the divide, among his friends and acquaintances Maria Giberne and Bowden's wife and children, Bowden himself having died in 1844. Among the more influential was Frederick Faber, at one time an Oxford don, then the Anglo-Catholic vicar of Elton, Huntingdonshire. He and some of the young men of his parish converted in November 1845.

The most important effect was to produce the break-up of the Oxford Movement. The most active of its leaders, intellectually and politically, having gone, its troops were in disarray. By no means all of its adherents crossed to Rome, but all were forced to reassess their positions. There was no shifting Keble and Pusey, and they were well prepared for Newman renouncing the Church of England. In May 1845 Keble had written to Sir John Coleridge debating what could be done 'by way of preparation for the blow', and asking, 'Does anything occur to you? I wish Pusey himself, Moberly, Marriott, and Manning etc., to apply themselves to the study of the controversy, for I am sure there will be great need of them.' Keble was ready to marshal many of the ablest minds in the Anglican Church to the defence of the faith.

For Newman, it was his *Essay on the Development of Christian Doctrine* which had finally led him across. His exploration of the history of Christianity persuaded him to believe that all things develop and change in time including the Church. It was not static. Both institutions and ideas, he realized, develop, and he gradually came to see that the Church of Rome had developed over the centuries into quite a different entity from what it was in Athanasius' time, but that the line of development was continuous. The Church of England was separate and had put itself out of communion with Rome, which was the centre of unity for the Catholic Church. Because ideas develop, so they had formed around for example, the Virgin Mary or the Papal Office; and as wise judgement is needed in the government of any organization or institution, so government through the apostolic office of the bishops with the Pope as head had developed. It was a collective responsibility. He saw, too, continued change and development in the future, yet the fact remained that the Church of Rome was continuous in history, and the Pope, St Peter's divinely appointed successor, was the centre of the Church's unity.

When Darwin's *On the Origin of Species* was published in 1859, it came as no particular surprise to Newman. His idea of history, with change and development implicit in it, enabled him to comprehend Darwin's claims, which shocked so many well-educated men whose minds were dominated by a static view of history: they believed in a literal exposition of the Book of Genesis, or at least thought that the world had been created in the form which they saw all round them. The famous debate at Oxford in 1860 between Bishop Samuel Wilberforce and T. H. Huxley, Darwin's defender, shows this. Newman's view of history was dynamic and he found no difficulty in reconciling his views to Darwin's. His interpretation of history was also revolutionary and disturbed many Roman Catholics, learned theologians among them, who adhered to the philosophy of St Thomas Aquinas.

Soon after Newman's conversion Wiseman, in whose vicariate Oxford lay, called him and the other friends from Littlemore to Oscott near Birmingham to be confirmed. The service took place on the Feast of All Saints, 1 November 1845. He recorded in his diary, 'Confirmed at 10 – with St John, Walker and Oakeley high mass afterwards Sermon dined at one had a talk with Wiseman.' While at Oscott with Wiseman he consulted him about the publication of the essay on 'Development'. In a letter to Dalgairns Newman reported his response, 'Dr W declined to see my Book . . .; "It is written before you joined the Church," he said – "the book is fact – I cannot alter it." Since that, two of his friends have persuaded him to send for it. Now since he is thus acted on by others against his judgment in one instance, why may he not in another?' A few days later, Wiseman relented and left the book uncensored; and so in its original state it was published.

Newman returned to Littlemore. The cottage property was his own and provided a retreat where he could ponder what his next moves would be. What role was he to play in the Church of Rome? Thoughts on this theme occupied him and reflected themselves in his correspondence. There was the problem of his followers, or 'disciples', the young men who had gone over to Rome with him from the Littlemore community. Newman felt a responsibility towards them and their futures. Wiseman had ideas. Newman wrote to Mrs Bowden from Littlemore, 'I want to be quiet here for some time, if I could, but the number of persons who wish to be employed and employed with me, makes it very difficult to be so. Dr Wiseman had

24. Cardinal Nicholas Wiseman, Rector
of the English College in Rome,
President of Oscott College. He was the
last Vicar Apostolic of the London
District and became the first Archbishop
of Westminster and a Cardinal in 1850.
Portrait by Henry Doyle

offered me the old Oscott College (about 2 miles from the Oscott) for a home – It has room for 20 to 30 persons.' He wrote that it was a tempting offer because 'my friends could get educated for orders etc. without separating from each other or from me'. He rounded off the letter, 'If we went to Oscott, our ultimate plan would be, partly to study and write, partly to educate, and partly to go about giving missions and helping the local clergy.' As early as 9 November 1845, then, there was some idea about the work which he and his friends would do, remarkably similar to that of his Oratorians later on.

At the same time he wondered what was most suitable for his talents. He wrote to 'Charissime' Dalgairns, that he and Ambrose St John felt more bound to London than Birmingham if they were destined to work with the poor, or the multitude in general: 'And again, my line has hitherto lain with educated persons, I have always had a fancy that I might be of use to a set of persons like the lawyers – or again I might be of use to the upper classes; now London is the only place for doing this in. London is a centre – Oxford is a centre – Brummagem is no centre.' The idea, nevertheless, of beginning with Oscott, and going on to a Congregation (he wondered whether he and St John might join the Jesuits) from which they could perform their work, was constantly in his mind, and it became clear that he should soon spend some time in Rome.

November 16 saw Faber received into the Roman Catholic Church at Oscott, but not before he had written to Newman asking him for advice. Enthusiastically, Faber proceeded to found a community for himself and his young men. He took the name of Brother Wilfrid and they became known as Wilfridians, but they were officially called the Brothers of the Will of God. Father Dominic Barberi, observing how much this group was dominated by Faber, later re-christened them Brothers of the Will of Faber.

Towards the end of November Newman visited a number of places, London, St Edmund's College, Ware, Oscott and Prior Park, near Bath, meeting old friends and finding new ones. Writing to St John from London he reported that the Pope had written a letter to Wiseman 'congratulating "Joannem Henricum Newman Puseistarum factionis ducem" on his recovery from heresy in which "misserime iacuerat".' From the seminary at Prior Park he wrote to friends about Wiseman's proposals: 'He distinctly stated that "he wished Old Oscott to be Littlemore continued" – this was "precisely his view". He wished laymen there – he wished anyone to be there who otherwise would have come to me. He wished it to be "a place of refuge".'

By the end of December the Oscott project was all but settled, and Newman was able to write to Richard Stanton that he was finding another name for the place so that letters would not miscarry. In the end he named the old college, Maryvale, which name it still has today.

The new year of 1846 required Newman to prepare for his removal from Littlemore, a sad experience since he knew it so well and so much had happened to him there. In one Christmas letter he confessed, 'You may think what a pain it is to quit this neighbourhood. I am now beginning my thirtieth year since my matriculation. Thus I have spent nearly two thirds of my life here.' He wrote to Henry Wilberforce, 'It is a sad thing to leave Littlemore – but one has no function, position, or occupation there – and one cannot stand all the day idle ... since we have made up our minds, I suppose we should begin packing up at once – but the house has to be put to rights before we get into it.' On 4 January he was able to report that the builders promised to get the old college ready in a month. Meanwhile he made other visits, to Faber at Birmingham, to Ratcliffe, the College of the Rosminians, near Loughborough, to Grace Dieu Manor, the residence of a prominent Catholic layman Ambrose Phillipps in Leicestershire, to York, Ushaw, Stonyhurst and Liverpool.

Finally, back at Littlemore, his diary entry for 20 February recorded, 'Packing finished.' He made his last round of calls on friends, on Sunday 22, 'went to Mass at St Clements for the last time', and then, 'Fly came for me and my baggage at 4 o'clock to take me to Johnson's for good and all.'

THE NEWMAN-OOTH COLLEGE &c.

AT LITTLEMORE NEAR OXFORD.

25. 'The Newman-ooth College'. A satire on Littlemore as a staging post to the Roman Catholic colleges of Maynooth, Ireland and Oscott, Birmingham. An 'Oxford' caricature. Such caricatures were sold by Oxford booksellers during the second half of the nineteenth century

Manuel Johnson, the Radcliffe Observer, whose house in Oxford was a meeting place for Tractarians, lodged him for his last night in Oxford, and Pusey visited him late that night. Subsequently, Newman and Johnson met only once although they continued to write to each other. The following day at half past eight in the morning, he and Bowles set out for Maryvale, where they were joined by St John, John Brande Morris, Stanton and John Walker. Thus the community was established, and Newman was not to return to Oxford for another thirty-two years. As he wrote in the *Apologia*, he was to see only its spires from the railway during that time.

It was Wiseman's intention that Newman should as soon as possible go to Rome, and as early as April 1846 Newman reported that plans were afoot. He informed Mrs Bowden that he was to go there at the end of June to the College of the Sacred Congregation of Propaganda, the institution responsible for the administration of territories which are not organized formally by the Roman Catholic Church, to prepare for ordination as a Roman Catholic priest. Doubts had plagued his conscience about this process because the Roman Church had never specifically condemned Anglican Orders: they had not been declared invalid. And repetition in the Church's view was sacrilege. He had been convinced in the end that the conditional administration of the Sacraments was admissible. He explained to Mrs Bowden, 'Thus Dr Bramston, late Bishop of the London District, received Roman orders twice, there being a doubt about the validity of the first administration. The Catholic authorities then treat Anglican orders, which they consider only doubtful, in no other way than they treat their own when doubtful.'

As it turned out, on Saturday 6 June he received 'tonsure and minor orders at Oscott with St John etc', and he admitted to Henry Wilberforce that he was relieved that his going abroad was put off until the autumn. Saturday 5 September eventually turned out to be the sailing date and as usual Newman was accompanied by St John. When St John joined Newman in London on Friday 4, he developed bad toothache and Newman recorded in his diary that St John had to have the tooth extracted: 'bleeding would not stop – his gum artery injured.' He was not fit until Monday when the pair set out for Brighton and thence to Dieppe.

They made their way in stages to Rome, by diligence to Rouen, by rail to Paris where they were met by Robert Coffin who had been Vicar of St Mary' Magdalen at Oxford. Newman had taken him when wavering in December 1845 to Prior Park where he was received into the Roman Church. At Besançon they lodged at Archbishop Mathieu's, and then they made for the Jura and Lausanne. They crossed by way of the Simplon Pass into Italy, St John noting that they walked the greater part of the way and arrived in Milan on 28 September. There they stayed in part of the priests' house next to the Church of St Fidelis. They had few introductions to people in Milan, since Wiseman seemed to know no one there, and yet Newman found he loved the city and especially the Duomo, its cathedral. He reported that the Duomo moved him more than St Peter's did in Rome. To John Walker, one of the Maryvale community, he wrote, 'The Duomo is the most beautiful building I ever saw. As you go about the city, its pinnacles are like bright snow against the blue sky. We have been up to the top twice. The Alps look fine from the top – especially Monte Rosa.'

On the day before he left Milan, having rested, for Rome, he reflected on his learning of a foreign language: he noted in his diary that it was like learning sanctity: 'How bad our pronunciation must be to the angels! and in learning a language one is better one day, worse another.' They set off for Pavia on 23 October. A day or two was spent in Genoa and from there they went by sea to Leghorn and diverted for a day to Pisa. Then, on again by steamer to Civita Vecchia, where they took a diligence to Rome arriving there on 28 October. The cost of the journey, including the five weeks' stay in Milan and fees for Italian lessons for three and a half weeks, amounted to £33 8s 9d. The following day, they were in St Peter's listening to the Pope celebrating Mass.

Unfortunately their rooms at the College of Propaganda were not ready

26. The chapel in Rome at the College of Propaganda where Newman first celebrated Mass, 1846

for them, still being papered and painted. They had to stay longer than they intended at Buys's Hotel, which was not at all to Newman's liking: 'It is a palace of filth . . . here (*ex uno disce omina*) the carpet is a nest of fleas and they have milk pans for slop pails.' Relief came when at last they moved into the College: 'We are certainly most splendidly lodged.' All the furniture and fittings were brand new and they ate well: 'We have two meat meals very good ones, at 11½ and 8, in fact dinners; a breakfast, caffe au lait, toast and butter (à l'Anglaise) at 7, and the Rector has determined we shall have tea some time in the evening.'

Newman described the College as one of the strictest schools in Rome. All the students were 'boys or youths' except for himself and St John, and they were of all nationalities. He wrote to Jemima that 'there are 32 languages spoken here, and the boys are made up of "Parthians and Medes and Elamites", Chinese, Negroes, Egyptians, Albanians, Germans, Irish, and Americans'. Fortunately for Newman, whose Italian was not all that good, the language of instruction was Latin.

On Sunday 22 November they were summoned quite unexpectedly to see the Pope. The weather had been consistently bad. Newman's diary reported day after day rain and bitter winds: both he and St John went down with colds. That Sunday was just such a rainy day, when the rector of the Collegio gave them half an hour's notice for presenting themselves to the Pope. As Newman told Frederick Bowles, it rained so hard that when they got back from walking to the College, their cloaks had 'a very deep fringe of the nastiest stuff I ever saw'. The rector was unperturbed by their state of dress: he was used to the problem: 'So the tails of our mantellas were dipped in water, not to remove, but to hide the colour of the dirt. (This was the simple fact, as next morning showed) and in this state we went in Monsignor Brunelli's carriage to be introduced to the Holy Father.' Pius IX struck Newman as a healthy, vigorous, middle-aged man who was kindly in countenance and manner. He was 'so familiar, that when he had told us some story about the conversion of an English clergyman, St John in his simplicity said "What is his name?" – at which he with great good humour laid his hand on his arm, and said something like "Do you think I can pronounce your English names?" or "Your English names are too much for me." He is quick in his movements and ran across the room to open a closet and give me a beautiful oil painting of the Mater Dolorosa.'

The Propaganda's style of dress for outdoors, either the mantella over a cassock, or a fareola over a clerical coat, shorts, buckles, and stockings, was inadequate safeguard from the mire of Rome's streets, or the cold. The hat was also ineffective. Newman described it as 'a stupendous triangular hat – so contrived as to be susceptible of every puff of wind, but cocked so high in front as to afford the face no protection against the sun.'

As January 1847 passed, the possibility gradually became more clearly defined in Newman's mind of establishing an oratory in England. The decision to do so proved a momentous step in his career. In the middle of the month he wrote to Dalgairns, 'The Oratorian Rule seems a sort of Deus ê machinâ here; and so Dr W [Wiseman] has wished it to be.' He pointed out the attractions of an Oratory and asked Dalgairns how he thought it would suit them all. They would have to give up Dominican notions of being teachers, 'of divinity in schools, or of classics or philosophy'; and they would have to be situated in a town. Oratorian duties had to take up only part of members' time: there would be nothing to prevent individuals from taking little part in the direct duties of the Oratory 'and devoting themselves to reading and writing'. Newman described how St Philip Neri met with his brethren for three hours each day, and anyone else who wanted to join them was welcome. He continued, 'On festivals it might also be, or at least embrace, the discussion which would be found in a mechanic's institute; indeed I should wish at any rate the Oratory to include the functions of a Mechanics' Institute among its duties.' He reckoned that the Oratory should be made up of about ten or twelve people, and he saw for his companions suitable individual tasks: 'there would be much time for reading etc. E.g. for Penny. It would be work in the *way* of reading. It would afford room for lecturing and disputation which may be *my* line – for preaching, which is (one of) *yours* – for taking care of young people, which is St John's. For science which may be Christie's, for music which is Formby's and Walker's. Though it does not embrace *schools* for high or low, or theology as such, it comes as near both as is possible without actually being either.' He finished by stating that although both he and St John felt London had particular claims on them, they would begin by opening such an Oratory in Birmingham: necessarily the project would need the backing of Wiseman, the Propaganda College, the Oratory in Rome, and indeed a Papal brief.

He saw in St Philip, the founder of the Roman Oratory, a reflection of Keble. Newman could never forget, nor ever stop admiring, Keble. He wrote to Jemima, 'This great Saint reminds me in so many ways of Keble, that I can fancy what Keble would have been, if God's will had been he should have been born in another place and age; he was formed on the same type of extreme hatred of humbug, playfulness, nay oddity, tender love for others, and severity, which are the lineaments of Keble.'

On Sunday 21 February Signor Brunelli, the Secretary of the Congregation of Propaganda, went to the Pope to seek his approval of Newman's plans. When he wrote to Mrs Bowden two days later Newman was able to report, 'The Pope has taken us up most warmly – offered us a house here for a noviciate, proposed others joining us here – and our going back together to England. I trust this plan would not keep us beyond the Autumn. It is no secret we are to be Oratorians.' This same news he passed on to his friends and confidants. To David Lewis, who had once been his curate at St Mary's and who converted in 1846, he wrote, 'We are to be children of St Philip Neri.' To Father Dominic Barberi, he wrote, 'We are to be Oratorians. The Pope has been very kind to us.'

In March it became apparent that Faber had heard the news that Newman and his friends, who were beginning to gather in Rome for their noviciate, were to become Oratorians. Faber, back in England, had removed himself and his Wilfridians from Birmingham to North Staffordshire where they ran a sort of mission, St Wilfrid's, under the patronage of the Earl of Shrewsbury. Faber had recently begun a series of translations of Italian lives of saints, and had developed a great admiration for St Philip Neri. He had even suggested to Dr Wiseman that he should form an Oratory: Wiseman had been unenthusiastic. Now Faber discovered that Newman had obtained authority to proceed with a plan which had for some time been in his own mind. He was naturally upset. He wrote to Newman that 'the news of your becoming an Oratorian of course raised a fresh little assault on us, as we ought to follow your example and merge into an old order'. He said that some old Catholics had suggested that the Wilfridians would feel themselves 'supplanted', and that 'in short – it seems that people think we are now in opposition to you'. Newman replied that there was no chance of a clash of interests: 'I repeat, there is not a chance of your and our interfering with each other. England is large enough – we have no preference for any town – Birmingham is nearest to us, that is all – and you have no particular connexion with Birmingham.' It was obvious from the start that Newman saw their rôles as separate; and that was the way, in the end, that the two were to work.

During April Newman and St John went into retreat at the Jesuit House of St Eusebio, prior to ordination. Newman wrote some notes in Latin during that time, which read as an exercise in humility and self-abnegation: 'I have in my mind a wound or cancer, the presence of which prevents me from being a good Oratorian. It cannot be described in a few words, for it is many-sided.' He analysed himself with admirable frankness: 'So far as I know I do not desire anything of this world; I do not desire riches, power or fame; but on the other hand I do not like poverty, troubles, restrictions, inconveniences.' He regretted that 'increasing years have deprived me of that vigour and vitality of mind which I once had and now have no more'. He confessed that the vigour of his faith had become dulled, that for some years he had fallen into a kind of despair and gloomy state of mind. His best years, he felt, had passed and he saw himself as fit for nothing, 'a useless log'. He thought his old cheerfulness had almost vanished, and lamented, 'My mind wanders unceasingly; and my head aches if I endeavour to concentrate upon a single subject.' Little did he realize what work lay in store for him.

At the end of May Newman and St John were ordained Deacons in St John Lateran, and one day later on Sunday 30 May they were ordained priests. Newman and some of his companions began their Oratorian novitiate. His diary for 28 June recorded that on that day he left the College of Propaganda for good and proceeded with six colleagues to Santa Croce, where they were to be under the direction of Father Rossi of the Rome Oratory. Later he was to confide that he found Father Rossi and Santa Croce 'dreary'.

27. Santa Croce in Rome where in 1847 Newman and Ambrose St John made their Oratorian novitiate

At the end of August they went to Naples where they spent a busy time visiting churches and sight-seeing. One day they went to Pompeii, and thence up Vesuvius getting home at 3.30 the next morning. Another day they walked up to Monte Cassino where they stayed overnight, then walked down to St Germano, and travelled by diligence back to Rome.

It was during this period, between the return to Rome and his departure for England, that Newman spent much of his time writing the largely autobiographical novel *Loss and Gain*, in which a young Oxford undergraduate converts to Roman Catholicism. It is at the same time both serious and amusing. Newman showed his hero Charles Reding working out his religious position against the background of mid-nineteenth century Oxford, the authentic background of Newman's own university days. Newman thoroughly enjoyed writing it: he said it often made him laugh. Many people, used to his sermons, tracts and learned essays, were most surprised by his lightness of touch, and some of his more single-minded critics pronounced that he had 'sunk lower than Dickens'.

On 10 October Newman wrote to Wiseman about the English Oratory, 'The Pope has appointed me first Superior, with power to choose four Deputies.' The statutes were to be those of the Rome Oratory, adapted for England by Newman, and he reported to Wiseman that they were settled and had gone to Press. Soon Newman and St John were ready and able to leave Rome and make for England. On 6 December they set out and on Christmas Eve landed in Dover. They went straight to London, staying at Hatchett's hotel, where on Christmas Day Newman said Mass at Mrs Bowden's private chapel.

By the end of December Newman was back at Maryvale ordering his affairs, and the beginning of 1848 found him seeing the proofs of *Loss and Gain* though the press. Since the novel was to be published anonymously, Newman and Burns, the publisher, used David Lewis as an intermediary with the printer. It was not until 1874 that Newman put his name to the text.

The main business of the year was to do with the establishment of the Oratory. February 1 saw the setting up of the Congregation. Newman recorded in his diary: 'First Vespers of the Purification set up the English Congregation of the Oratory admitting 9–5 Fathers – 1 novice – 3 lay brothers.' The fathers included St John, Dalgairns, Penny, Coffin and Stanton. Two of the lay brothers came from Faber's 'Brothers of the Will of God'. Two days later Newman wrote to Mrs Bowden announcing his intention of admitting Faber and his friends to the Oratory at St Wilfrid's on the fourteenth of that month. In the meantime the Oratorians had started their work: 'We have begun to take duty in Birmingham – that is, to assist the Priests at St. Chad's.'

On 14 February Faber and his Brothers were admitted Oratorians. Only Faber and Hutchinson were then priests. The others were Austin Mills, Alban Wells and Nicholas Darnell. Eleven lay brothers were also admitted.

Almost immediately problems began to arise with Lord Shrewsbury who had clear ideas about the responsibility which the Wilfridians owed to himself and St Wilfrid's. Newman wrote diplomatically to him about the future of the mission, which was near Cheadle, 'We see our way so little at present, that I am not able to speak about Cheadle. Certainly the wish at Rome was that we should place ourselves in the large towns, such as Birmingham, London and Manchester.' The main trouble was that Lord Shrewsbury and the Wilfridians, especially Hutchinson, had sunk a great deal of money into the St Wilfrid's venture, and Shrewsbury was unwilling to see his investment wasted and his intention of having his church served by a religious community thwarted. Hutchinson saw the problem in these terms: either St Wilfrid's had to be given up, because it was unsuitable for Oratorians, and £7,000 which had been spent on it lost, or the Oratory had to take over St Wilfrid's and be obliged to evangelize the locality according to Shrewsbury's wishes. He saw a solution in Newman's party, the other two parties concerned being the Wilfridians and Shrewsbury, giving ground and agreeing to move the Oratory to St Wilfrid's. Shrewsbury's generosity would not then be slighted, and the Wilfridians' investment of £7,000 would not have proved futile. There was no possibility of the Oratorians being able to afford the upkeep of both Maryvale and St Wilfrid's, so that Maryvale would have to be sacrificed.

In the end, that is what happened, and on the last day of October the Oratorians moved to St Wilfrid's. Newman did not see this as a permanent solution, but acquiesced for the moment, while still recognizing the need for Oratories to exist in major towns and cities. He wrote in November to David Lewis, 'As to the London Oratory, this must be our *end*, guiding all our attempts to gain one – to place ourselves where we are likely to influence the "ordo honestior, cultior, doctior". As to the poor, there are plenty in Birmingham or Liverpool – the thing which brings us to London, is the upper class. Any position which makes that a secondary object, has no temptation for us.' Once again from Newman's remarks, it is clear that he saw his own vocation as an Oratorian among the more respectable of society who were no less in need of spiritual help than the poor. His own experience, particularly at Oxford, he felt fitted him for this.

In Birmingham Newman found a site for his city Oratory in a disused gin distillery at Alcester Street. In London, an arrangement to take over a building in Bayswater fell through, but the search continued.

The Vicar Apostolic of the Midland District was William Ullathorne who was to become Bishop of Birmingham in 1850. During 1848 Newman and he became closely involved in a controversy over Faber's translation of the *Lives of the Saints*. In October Newman wrote to Faber, telling him that several houses had been visited and seen in Birmingham as possible sites for the Birmingham Oratory; he went on, 'I am anxious about the Saints' Lives. There is a row blowing up.' He expressed reservations about Faber's decision to publish the Life of St Rose of Lima first. Some old Catholics criticized the series immediately because it concentrated on Italian, French and Spanish saints, and because many of the lives contained extravagant accounts of miracles and austerities, and some revealed scandals in Catholic countries. Newman was guarded about whether or not the Oratorians should take over the publication of *The Lives*, and postponed making up his mind. Before the year ended, a severe review appeared in *Dolman's Magazine* condemning the Life of St Rose: it attacked Faber in person and held that he and his translation were guilty of promoting, 'gross, palpable idolatry.' It was not sufficient for *Dolman's* editor that each of *The Lives* had the imprimatur in its country of origin, nor that the project had the approval of Ullathorne's predecessors in the Central District. Newman realized that the Oratory could not now adopt them, without Ullathorne's approval, because they had come under attack publicly: he advised caution and suspension. *The Lives* then found many influential supporters, which made Ullathorne defensive, and produced an apology for the hostile review from Edward Price, the editor of *Dolman's*. Eventually after Newman had demonstrated his support for Faber (he wrote for example not only to Ullathorne, but to Wiseman and Newsham, President of Ushaw College, defending the passage in St Rose), Ullathorne approved the series and publication was resumed at the beginning of 1849 under the auspices of the English Oratory.

On 26 January Newman travelled to Birmingham, to set up the Oratory in Alcester Street. All the bits and pieces of personal and Oratory possessions were conveyed there with difficulty. Newman described the journey to Robert Coffin, whom he had appointed Rector in charge of St Wilfrid's. There was amid much else a large basket of vials and gallipots, a violin and case, a box of relics, a plaster Madonna, a saucer of China shells: 'My fly was filled nearly to the top, and it's a wonder how I got in among them, a greater how I got out, and the greatest how everything was not smashed by the jogging.' On 2 February, the anniversary of the founding of the English Oratory, the chapel was opened, and at once the Oratorians started their pastoral work among Birmingham's poor. Interest in the Alcester Street venture was proved by the large crowd which turned out for Newman's first sermon at the chapel-opening service. Some five to six hundred attended without any disturbance.

28. The first Birmingham Oratory, formerly a distillery and subsequently a school, taken over by Newman in 1849

Faber remained behind at St Wilfrid's as novice-master, and immediately affairs there began to develop unsatisfactorily. There were several elements involved. Faber said that many left behind at St Wilfrid's were unhappy at the separation. The novices complained of Newman's 'coldness' towards them. He hinted at a dislike of St John, and a resentment of Newman's 'particular' friendship with him. In retrospect, although Newman spent much time in writing to individual novices and settling their minds, most of the complaints seem to have been Faber's own. On top of all this Faber expressed his impatience to found a London house of the Oratory, in which scheme there was an inherent difficulty. Faber did not cease to submit himself to Newman and continually swear never to desert him, and yet he felt that the Oratory ought to be in London. He saw there the purpose of the Congregation as twofold: Newman would minister to the educated and wealthy, and in particular to converts, while Faber himself would carry out missions in the church to a wider public. Newman, on the other hand, felt the Birmingham Oratory to be most important, and thought that if he did not continue it, no one would. In addition, he had grown fond of Ullathorne, recognized his allegiance to him, and was most unwilling to desert him.

In April Newman decided to secure premises for the London Oratory at King William Street (now William IV Street), the Strand. He wrote to

29. F. W. Faber, convert, and first Superior of the London Oratory. A daguerreotype from the 1850s

Faber on the 22nd: 'Yesterday I wrote to you agreeing to take a 21 years lease of the K William Street House at £400 – the price is enormous, but I dare say not too much for London. I have not said a kind or encouraging word to you all thro' this letter, but I am busy till I am stupid. How I should like to see you.'

A little later he informed Coffin that Faber was to be 'the acting Superior of the London House. He has submitted to a year and a half's subordination, and to take the lead is his proper place.' On 31 May the London Oratory was founded. Wiseman preached in the morning and Newman in the afternoon.

Newman wrote a memorandum on the division of the Oratory, dated 31 May. It stated that the Congregation determined to colonize from Birmingham to London and listed what those going to London would give up, for example, the Mother Oratory, vestments and Church plate, a library; but they would gain certain things, 'the Metropolis, the centre of political and ecclesiastical influence, instead of factory youths and snobbish intellects'. The real problem was what to do with St Wilfrid's. Newman proposed that it should be maintained financially in the future by both Houses. It continued to be difficult and in the end it was decided that a school should be set up there. That proved impracticable, and finally it was transferred to the Passionist Order.

Although Faber was Acting Superior of the London Oratory, Newman was Superior of the whole Congregation and had to manage London affairs the best he could from a distance, putting up with Faber's inconsistent and sometimes eccentric behaviour. Newman was concerned that both Oratorian communities should include 'born' Catholics as well as converts, and consequently he welcomed two priests of Irish origin, Robert Whitty and James McQuoin from St Edmund's, Ware. Faber could not get on with them and their own hesitation in committing themselves led to their departure. Faber, showing considerable prejudice, described McQuoin as 'fickle and shilly shallying'. He remarked that 'weakness and treachery are next door to each other; in an Hibernian they are synonyms,' and that if Newman could not manage McQuoin 'how much less I! Why, even the civility of an Irishman riles me . . .'

Faber clearly had the sort of personality which attracted people to him, but his character was not stable enough to manage people amicably in a community. There is no doubt that his energy and resourcefulness did much to make the London Oratory a success, but Newman continually had to advise him and restrain him. Those under him often lost patience, and Newman had to mediate and make peace between them.

It was necessary, too, for Newman to remind the London community occasionally that they should devote some time to literary and intellectual pursuits as well as to missionary work. Newman himself was able to write and publish in October 1849 *Discourses to Mixed Congregations*. The month previously, he and St John had amongst many other duties gone to minister to cholera patients at Bilston as the epidemic abated, in order to give the parish priest some relief. Typically enough, the theme of the *Discourses* was the war fought by the spirit of Christ against the selfishness of the world.

By the end of 1849 the Oratorians were immensely popular at Alcester Street, a fact which aroused in Ullathorne some suspicions. For a long time he was not convinced that a group of converts, in spite of having Rome's credentials, could possibly be a proper religious community. At this particular time he never gave Newman the title of Father, always calling him Mr Newman. Newman did not think it important and said that he supposed by the same application 'he speaks of Mr Dominic'.

Newman published in the following year, 1850, *Twelve Lectures on Difficulties felt by Anglicans in submitting to the Catholic Church*, which were directed at people who had taken part in the Oxford Movement. He explained the aim of the volume in the preface, 'to give fair play to the conscience by removing those perplexities in the view of catholicity which keep the intellect from being touched by its agency, and give the heart an excuse for trifling with it.'

In the August of that year Newman's diary recorded that 'Dr Ullathorne admitted me into the doctorate, which had been sent me from Rome, and supped with us'. The Church of Rome had completed its assimilation of him and made him one of her divines. He admonished Mrs Bowden though, 'Don't direct to me as "Dr," please, but Father, which is my proper title – I don't know myself in so strange a dress.' The immediate follow-up was what has come to be known as the papal aggression, the establishment of the new Catholic Hierarchy in England. This matter had arisen at the time of Newman's stay in Rome, and was something which Wiseman was closely concerned with.

In 1850 Wiseman was called to Rome for elevation to the cardinalate and a territorial hierarchy in England was set up under him. George Talbot, one of Pius IX's chamberlains, wrote to Newman, 'I tell you in confidence that I have done all I could to induce the Pope to allow Dr Wiseman to return to England as Cardinal Archbishop.' This he was to do, and prior to his return he sent on to England a pastoral letter entitled, 'From out the Flaminian Gate', which celebrated in triumphal language

30. Interior of the London Oratory Church, *c* 1865

31. 'Mr. Newboy holding up Mr. Wiseboy's tail' from a *Punch* cartoon of 1850

the restoration of the Roman Catholic Church to its true 'orbit in the ecclesiastical firmament'. Naturally enough there was extreme resentment from the English establishment. *The Times* of 14 October published a violent attack on 'the new-fangled Archbishop of Westminster'. Wiseman's Acting Vicar-General, Whitty, although he realized that the letter would fan the flames of agitation, had the letter read in all Roman Catholic Churches. *The Times* pressed home its attack and the other newspapers followed. They considered Queen Victoria insulted by Wiseman's language and interpreted the institution of the hierarchy as an attempt to dominate the English people. Lord John Russell, the Prime Minister, issued a public letter denouncing the Catholic Church's 'pretension of supremacy over the realm of England'. The Protestant opposition moved into place, and soon there were anti-Popery riots, wrecking of buildings and attacks on priests. *Punch* became so anti-Catholic that its leading artist Doyle, who had listened to Newman's lectures on Anglican difficulties in the lower chapel of King William Street, left the magazine. Its cartoons cruelly held a thin, emaciated, bespectacled Newman and a fat, hypocritical Wiseman, responsible for the present troubles. Puseyites came in for particular criticism: they were felt to be traitors in the camp. There was, after all, the example of Newman and his friends going over to Rome. The following year more fuel was found for this particular fire when Newman was called to Leeds to receive nearly all the clergy of St Saviour's Church which had been built by Pusey as a memorial to his wife and daughter Lucy.

Wiseman tried to calm the storm when he arrived in Westminster and published 'An Appeal to the English People' in all the leading news-papers. He tried to make clear, and reassure people, that the Hierarchy made no designs on temporal power: it existed merely to exercise spiritual care of Roman Catholics.

In London Faber and the Oratorians were particularly involved, and were made obvious in going their rounds by their distinctive dress. Faber told of how abuse was hurled at them by gentlemen from carriage win-dows. On 5 November it was feared the House would be burned down, but the mob made do with burning effigies of the Pope and cardinals. In all this, Faber was very much on his own, for the London House had separated from the Birmingham Oratory on 9 October: it was now an autonomous Oratory. The decree releasing the London Oratorians and allowing for their independence read in part that the Fathers of the Oratory in Birmingham, 'with much regret and with sorrowful hearts, set free from connexion with our body, our dear brothers and intimate friends', who were Faber, Dalgairns, Coffin, Stanton, Hutchinson, Knox, Alban Wells and Philip Gordon.

Newman saw clearly the benefits of the new hierarchy. He wrote to Talbot that the church should not give way to fears, 'Fear is the worst of counsellors. We must not retreat a foot.' He pointed out, 'One great advantage of the erection of the Hierarchy and the coming of the Cardinal is that it *will force us* to have Canonists, theologians, men of business, and men of savoir faire.'

The popular attacks went on into the new year of 1851. It had even been rumoured that Newman was married and had locked his wife away in a convent.

The anti-Popery agitation prompted the Evangelical Alliance to marshal all possible forces against Roman Catholics. It found an agent for its work in an ex-Dominican monk called Giacinto Achilli who spoke bitterly against the Catholic Church, telling stories of the Roman Inquisi-tion before which he had been brought for a series of crimes against morality. Travelling the country, Achilli lectured in Birmingham which brought him particularly to Newman's notice. Newman decided to offset his influence and used his fifth lecture on 'The Present Position of Cath-olics in England', a series he was delivering at the Birmingham Corn Exchange, to denounce Achilli. Newman enumerated the various immoralities of Achilli, basing his lecture mainly on a well-documented account of the Dominican's transgressions which Wiseman had written for the *Dublin Review* in 1850.

It became clear at the end of August 1851, that Achilli, encouraged by the Evangelical Alliance, intended to set in motion an action for libel. Newman hastily sent to Wiseman for his documents which substantiated the *Dublin Review* article, and to Talbot in Rome for evidence from the Inquisition and from any other quarters which would prove Achilli a rogue. Unfortunately neither realized just how urgent the business was. On 4 November Sir Frederick Thesiger and Sir Fitzroy Kelly, retained for Achilli, moved against Newman in court. The Attorney-General, Sir Alexander Cockburn, acted for Newman. Achilli, on oath, denied all the charges made against him by Newman and on 21 November the rule bringing Newman to trial was made absolute. He was seriously handicapped because neither Wiseman's documents, nor Talbot's collection of evidence from Rome, had reached him. He was naturally dejected, and wrote to Archbishop Cullen of Armagh, 'The Judges are against me, and a Protestant bias pervades the whole Court. It seems certain I cannot get the justice which a Protestant would, though this must not be said publicly.' He wrote to St John, 'The Judges are clean against me – will grant nothing – determined to bring on a trial and to have witnesses in the box instead of affidavits, the people present humming assent.'

There was no possibility of compromise and in any case Newman became convinced that the integrity of the Church demanded that a stand should be made against Achilli. In London an influential group of bishops and laymen organized the collection of funds for the expenses of the trial. Friends such as Joseph Gordon, an Oratorian, and Maria Gilberne were despatched to collect further evidence and witnesses against Achilli. The latter proved most difficult since it was uncertain when the trial would take place and how long it would last. These witnesses, Italian peasant folk, gathered in Paris and Maria Gilberne and St John had to organize entertainments for them. Achilli knew only too well the great difficulty in securing witnesses against him and maintaining them, and his lawyers manoeuvred to delay the legal proceedings.

At last the trial took place from 21 to 24 June 1852, and on the last day the jury decided that Newman had failed to prove his charges. There was great disappointment, but Newman refused to be too downcast. He wrote to Mrs Bowden, 'There is no doubt I have justified myself morally, in the eyes of everyone – and, though the party who uphold Achilli will call it a triumph, no one else but will call it, not a triumph for *him*, but simply a triumph over *me*.' *The Times* strongly criticized both the trial and the verdict, and censured the Judge, Lord Campbell: 'Who can hope to be believed when such a mass of evidence has been flung aside as worthless? We consider that a great blow has been given to the administration of justice in this country, and Roman Catholics will have henceforth only too good reason for asserting, that there is no justice for them in cases tending to arouse the Protestant feelings of judges and juries.'

On 21 November Sir Alexander Cockburn demanded a new trial.

Newman had been against the proposal as extending the whole business and keeping the final judgement still in suspense; but his lawyers persuaded him to agree. The demand threw the Court into consternation. Newman described to Joseph Gordon how Cockburn acted, 'Then he began a most masterly exposure of Judge and Jury, till there was a loud cheering from the audience, which was of course instantly put down. The Judges have allowed the matter to be argued.' In the event, a re-trial was not allowed, and on the last day of January 1853, Newman was sentenced to a fine of £100 and imprisonment until the fine was paid. Naturally it was paid immediately by his friends, but Newman had to endure a lecture from the Judge, Sir John Coleridge, Keble's friend and biographer. As Newman wrote to Bowles, 'Those opinions which we have heard are to the effect that I have gained a victory. I had a most horrible jobation from Coleridge – the theme of which was "deterioration". I *had* been one of the brightest lights of Protestantism – he had delighted in my books – he had loved my meek spirit etc.' To Sister Imelda Poole he wrote that Coleridge had said, 'I had been everything good when I was a Protestant – but I had fallen since I was a Catholic.'

The fine might have been small, but the expenses were great and finally amounted to over £14,000. They were defrayed by public subscription organized by Newman's many friends and admirers: many foreign Catholics contributed to the fund. One example of financial support came from Cullen: he wrote to Newman on 4 February, sending him £1,830 collected by the Dublin Committee of the Achilli trial fund, and remarked, 'The subscriptions are from every part of Ireland, and from every class of people. There are some other sums promised or collected.' In the end he sent a further £379.

Achilli left quickly for America, knowing no doubt that he had lost the moral battle. The expenses of the trial were settled. Newman constantly prayed for his benefactors, and out of the money left over, so generous were the contributions, Newman paid for the building of his university church in Dublin.

Chapter 6   The Irish University and rejection 1854–62

'Say not the struggle naught availeth,
The labour and the wounds are vain...'   A. H. Clough

The Achilli trial brought Newman troubles, worries, and an anxious suspense since the outcome of the proceedings was so protracted. Amid all this trouble, Newman's other duties continued and became particularly onerous. The Birmingham Oratory demanded its usual routine and much of Newman's attention. He was organizing the building of a new Oratory house at Edgbaston. It was widely rumoured that the cellars which were being dug for this building were to be used for murders. The accusation was made in Parliament, and naturally aroused great hostility within the local community. Fears had to be allayed and tempers cooled.

At the same time the London Oratory caused great difficulty. Newman was constantly consulted about London matters and even when the Oratories were made independent of each other in October 1850, Newman still kept certain overall powers of control which meant that he was at the mercy of Faber's confidences, enquiries, demands and even of his resentments. Faber had been elected Superior of the London Oratory. Newman wrote his congratulations on 13 October 1850, 'I congratulate your Very-reverence on your establishment as a House at St Philip and on your own elevation in particular.'

Faber's rule was not an early success. Like Newman in Birmingham, he had plans for moving his Oratory to a better site. He had designs on land at Brompton. Increasingly his fellow Oratorians found his ways intimidating and annoying. He did not respect others' confidences and proved erratic in his plans. His temperament was not improved by physical illness and in 1851 he fell prone to headaches and other pains in various limbs which doctors were unable to help him with but about which he complained to Newman. During September he was suffering pains in both wrists, which were diagnosed as gout. Newman pointedly remarked, 'I should almost be glad your ailments took a tangible shape like gout.' By the middle of October he was in a state of near collapse and wrote to Newman, 'Mr Tegart is apprehensive about the state of my brain, from long excitement and overwork, and insists on my leaving the Congregation for not less than 6 months, or he won't answer for it.' On 15 October Fathers Hutchinson and Dalgairns visited Newman to discuss Faber's plans for going to the Continent. Newman was concerned about Faber. He wrote to Stanton, 'It is a great evil, he cannot control his mental

32. The Birmingham Oratory. The buildings in the Italian renaissance style, by Henry Clutton, date from the 1860s. The domed Oratory Church of The Immaculate Conception was built as a memorial to Cardinal Newman, 1903–9

activity – else, to a certainty he will wear himself out. Who is Mr Tegart? is he an oracle? He has found out two new complaints in F. Wilfrid, gout and insanity.' In the end Newman's diary reported, 'F. Wilfrid set off for Jerusalem'. His plans changed, however, and he went to Italy. Foreign travel proved no palliative and he soon decided to return home, which brought alarm and confusion to the London Oratory. Dalgairns wrote a letter to Newman, now lost, which apparently listed many deficiencies of Faber's rule and gave Newman the impression that Dalgairns and others wanted Faber deposed. It produced a long reply from Newman emphasizing that they had chosen Faber for three years, 'no intolerable period – if it be a trial, you must get him to teach you to bear it. Everything will go wrong, even as a matter of calculation, if you depose F. Wd. It will be like private judgement and like waters running out.' Newman encouraged Dalgairns, 'You must not droop. I feel this strongly. You tend to make matters worse than they are. Beware of this.'

Dalgairns did not reply until much later, towards the end of December, when he made it clear that Newman had mistaken his intention. Hutchinson had wanted Newman to ask Faber to resign on the grounds of ill health. There was a strong disgust at Faber's restlessness. Hutchinson thought Faber was overbearing and interfered too much and too often. Dalgairns thought Faber consulted everybody too much, 'He consults us; he is opposed and then he chafes and is irritated … He brooks no opposition.' Newman had to make the peace and try to keep it. He wrote to Hutchinson on 28 December, 'I must say I wish I had power over him – but a physician surely has.' A plan evolved by which Faber should travel to America. Hutchinson approved and reported on how the London Oratory had fared since Faber had been away, 'I think very well on the whole – there have been no rows.' Both Hutchinson and Dalgairns agreed that if Faber were not any better than when he went, he should not be allowed to stay at the Oratory.

Newman wrote to Faber an 'ungracious' letter expressing 'sorrow' at his return, 'The truth is I have been fuming ever since you went, at the way you have been going on.' He had not obeyed his doctor, as St Philip had done. Tegart had prescribed six months: Faber had ignored 'one of the few opportunities as Father Superior has for obedience'. In the face of all advice, Faber refused to go abroad again, but moved to a country house at Hither Green, near Lewisham. He wrote about Newman to Stanton who was in Malta, 'The Padre has lost a front tooth and is looking old. He has clearly suffered a great deal about the trial, and he is like a regular quaint old saint about it.' By 23 January 1852 Hutchinson was able to inform Newman that he definitely thought Faber should continue as Superior: rest had strengthened him, and 'he so completely in every sense outweighs the rest of us.' Whereas the burden of acting for Faber had weakened Dalgairns. The recovery of Faber was to mean a restitution of his supremacy for the moment and an increase in friction between the two Oratories a little later.

Another important affair, which occupied Newman's mind during the time of his defence against Achilli's onslaught, was the setting up of a Catholic University in Ireland. In mid-July 1851 Archbishop Cullen had visited Birmingham and invited Newman to become the first Rector of the University to be established in Dublin. In retrospect, in 1870, Newman wrote that he had told Cullen he was willing to perform the duties of President or Rector although he would rather have been Prefect of Studies, 'I felt such an office as the latter would commit me less to an institution which had its seat in another country, and which on that account threatened, if I had the highest post in it, to embarrass my duties to the Birmingham Oratory.' It is clear that although the work of a university suited him, he was most anxious for it not to interfere with that of the Oratory which held his first loyalty. He wrote to Cullen later that month informing him that the Fathers of the Oratory thought he should be nothing less than Rector of the new University, 'under the notion that since I am their Superior, I ought not to have a subordinate place elsewhere.' He went on to say, 'I do not feel this *at all* myself – and I hope you will over rule it by showing them what the way of doing things is at Rome. But since they urge me, I write to you on the subject.' He ended by remarking, 'What I should desire is, to do as much work for the University as possible with *as little absence as possible* from this place.'

Newman's reluctance to give himself wholly to the University was not a happy sign for the success of the new venture; but Cullen was determined to have him. He sent a donation to the Oratory and according to James Hope said to him that, 'If we once had Dr Newman engaged as president, I would fear for nothing. After that everything would be easy.' Everything was far from easy. The other Oratory Fathers insisted that 'it is infra dig in the F. Superior of an Oratory', being anything less than head of the University; and at the same time Newman had distinctly divided loyalties. In addition there were many other troubles: the University was not recognized by the state, the Irish Bishops were suspicious both of it and Newman, and his organizing abilities were not at their best when occupied twice over.

Nevertheless he went to Ireland from 30 September to 8 October, spending most of his time at Thurles where the sub-committee on the organization of the University sat. Later he wrote his ideas to Cullen and commented that if he had the first appointment he feared he would take too much of an English and convert element to the new institution: it would 'create remark' and cause bad feeling. Newman thought that Thurles was quite unsuitable for the site of the University and proposed Dublin to which Cullen agreed. Then in the midst of all the worry of Achilli's charges, and the hard work of collecting evidence against him, on 12 November Newman wrote in his diary, 'Appointed Head of the new Catholic University.' The scheme was sanctioned by the Holy See and backed by the deliberations of the hierarchy of Ireland. Newman thought that it must succeed. As he wrote expressing his pleasure and gratitude as well as his anxiety about the attendant responsibilities, he commented to Cullen that the 'Achilli matter is a great annoyance'.

In 1852, just before the Achilli trial, he delivered in Dublin, between 10 May and 7 June, the first five lectures on University Education. There was to be no relief. Almost immediately the trial began, after which he again travelled to Dublin for the installation of Cullen as Archbishop of Dublin on 29 June: Cullen had been translated from Armagh. Back in England he preached before the Synod of the new hierarchy at Oscott his sermon known as 'The Second Spring'. As the Synod ended he heard of his sister Harriett's death. Troubles flocked to him. He wrote to Mrs Bowden, 'You may think how tried I am at this moment with my sister's death' and confided, 'Where I feel most *practically* the pain, is, that my Lectures in Dublin require, at my age, all the steam I can put on – and this affliction, coming upon the Achilli affair, pulls me down so much, that nothing but God's grace can keep me up. You must indeed pray for me, as I for you.' From 21 July to 20 November he composed the rest of the 'Discourses on the Scope and Nature of University Education': they were published the following February. He wrote to Richard Stanton at the end of that month, 'I hear my new volume is selling well. 150 copies have gone to Australia.'

The latter part of November 1852 was taken up with Sir Alexander Cockburn's application for a new trial in the Achilli affair. His demand, which Newman was doubtful of, brought many accompanying worries and consequently by the end of the month he was worn out. It was arranged that he should take a vacation with James Hope at Abbotsford, Sir Walter Scott's old seat; Hope had married Scott's granddaughter and was to change his name to Hope-Scott in 1853. Newman planned to travel by way of Ushaw and Durham. On 9 December he had to write to Hope that he was laid up with an attack of influenza 'sharper than perhaps I have ever had it.' He still intended to reach Hope by the 17th, since he was convalescent. He told him, 'At present it has taken the shape of lumbago, but I trust that will not last. The weakness is what I fear now, for I have been badly prostrated.'

By 11 pm on the 17, his diary reports, he was with Hope and his stay there gave him some timely rest, although domestic Oratorian problems pursued him.

The next year, 1853, was no less busy, nor less troubled for Newman, and in October he was at last summoned to Ireland to establish the Catholic University. The summons came from the University Committee at which only two bishops were present. Most of the Irish bishops were suspicious of the scheme and thought it too exclusively associated with Archbishop Cullen. Cullen seemed to drag his feet and towards the end of the year Newman was writing to Cullen making it plain that he should have a 'warrant' to set up the University endorsed by the Archbishop himself. If the scheme was to be initially successful, it needed public recognition.

Early in January 1854 Cullen started actively supporting Newman's ideas, but even more important was Cardinal Wiseman's manoeuvring in Rome where he suggested to Pius IX that Newman should be given a new brief for the University, which would confirm him as Rector and give him power to appoint tutors and lecturers; and, with Cullen's knowledge, he asked that Newman should be made a bishop to give him status and authority in Ireland. In retrospect Newman wrote that he had never wished for a bishopric, 'but that so it was, I did feel glad, for I did not see, without some accession of weight to my official position, I could overcome the inertia or opposition which existed in Ireland'.

Cullen changed his mind, thinking Newman a bishop would not be good for Ireland. He thought it would make a fuss and not please the Irish bishops. In Belgium, the Rector Magnificus was not a bishop; and there would be the expense of maintaining another bishopric. But news of the proposed elevation got out: Ullathorne, pleased with the prospect, had made it public in Birmingham. Newman was left in more suspense, for none of those men of eminence who had first seen the importance of his promotion in the ranks of the hierarchy ever explained to him why the proposal was never carried out.

In February Newman visited a number of Irish bishops to secure their support for the University, and although expectant of news from Rome when the synod of Irish bishops met in March to discuss the building of the University, not a word was said about Newman becoming a bishop. In the end Newman saw the omission as advantageous, since it would allow him more easily to break away from the University to return to his Oratory than if he were elevated.

The problem of fulfilling two rôles dogged him. He confided to Ambrose St John, who was to be Rector of the Oratory in his place, just after his installation as Rector of the new University on 4 June, 'The Archbishop ended with a touching address to me. How I am to continue in Birmingham (entre nous) turns my head.' His dual responsibilities meant that he had to travel backwards and forwards between Birmingham and Dublin for the next few years and the Oratory was still to take up much of his time. A month later he returned to Birmingham and bought land for a retreat house and cemetery for the Oratory at Rednal.

In Dublin he secured the lease of 6, Harcourt Street, named St Mary's House. There he resided and on 3 November the University was opened. A few days later he delivered the inaugural lecture for the School of Philosophy and Letters. The next months were concerned in making sure that the University Gazette which he instituted did not founder, in collecting and appointing staff, in trying to have Cullen ratify appointments, and collaborating with John Hungerford Pollen in designing and building the University Church.

In the autumn of 1854 Cullen had gone to Rome to defend himself against Irish nationalist opponents such as Frederick Lucas and Archbishop MacHale. He advised Newman against the Young Irelanders among whom were some of the most able, aspiring Irishmen. Newman, for the most part, got on well with them and was unwilling to bar them from teaching posts because of their politics. Cullen was deeply offended by Newman's refusal to heed his warnings and from then on relations between the two men deteriorated. Cullen, who had been the prime mover of the University, failed to co-operate. The University, already without the support of the Irish episcopacy, lost the support of the Primate. Newman's letters to Cullen went unanswered and he was frustrated at every turn. He wanted influential laymen to give financial security to the

33. Newman House and the University Church, Dublin. He founded the original Catholic University of Ireland in Dublin in 1853

University, and help in its complicated administration. Again this proposal for a committee of laymen caused offence. He wrote to Cullen asking him to endorse, among other appointments, Pollen's as Professor of Fine Arts. Almost a month later he informed Pollen, 'Some weeks back, when I found that Dr Cullen's delay was protracted, I wrote to him to mention your name for the office which you were kind enough to allow me to impose upon you. He has not yet answered me.' In the same letter, he showed that he had decided to proceed with the plan for a University Church without Cullen's advice since he had not heard from him.'

While Newman was busily trying to establish additional faculties, make friends for the University, and journeying to and from England, Cullen began to doubt the value of the whole project and Newman's appointment as Rector in particular. In October 1855 Cullen wrote to Tobias Kirby, the Rector of the Irish College in Rome, an important letter which Propaganda accepted. It ran:

With regard to the university, we have done nothing. For more than three months Father Newman has been in England, and has left a convert Englishman named Scratton here to take his place. To the Vice-Rector he gave no instructions. I have not therefore been able to find out how things stand, but they don't seem to me to be going in a way that can be defended. The continued absence of the Rector cannot be approved.

He complained about lack of discipline: young men were allowed to go out at all hours, and to smoke; they had no fixed times for study. He thought Newman did not attend to details and hoped for a 'system' to be introduced. He analysed the main problem: 'It is true we shall always have the difficulty that "Nemo potest duobus dominis servire", (no one is able to serve two houses), and Father Newman cannot be excepted. He cannot spend a great part of the year in England and govern a university here. I hope they won't make him a bishop in Rome until he has properly arranged all the affairs of the university.'

Newman was not blind to the difficulties. He had always maintained that both Englishmen and converts would cause resentment, but he knew that the institution had to be got going. He wrote at the end of August to Mrs Bowden, 'It is swimming against the stream, to move at all – still we are in motion.' He told her that the medical schools were to open that October and the Church was being built. Four years had been spent: the Pope had given him two more years leave of absence. It was just as well he did not know the extent to which Cullen was undermining him. He knew his own deficiencies; 'A Rector ought to be a more showy, bustling man than I am, in order to impress the world that we are great people ... I ought to dine out every day, and of course I don't dine out at all. I ought to mix in literary society and talk about new gasses and the price of labour – whereas I can't recollect what I once knew, much less get up a whole lot of new subjects – I ought to behave condescendingly to others, whereas they are condescending to me – And I ought above all to be 20 years younger, and take it up as the work of my life.'

It is curious that when he did come to resign the University Rectorship, both Cullen and the Irish bishops were dismayed. His loss was only to be realized as he was about to be gone. By the autumn of 1856 he had decided that he would keep to his decision to leave the University in the autumn of the following year. The University Church had been opened on 1 May, the synod of bishops confirmed Newman's appointments and the statutes for three years, but increasingly Newman felt he was needed back in Birmingham. His first duty lay with the Oratory, and his task in the University was made no easier than before by waning support from English Catholics, distrust among the Irish laity, and what he termed the 'impracticability' of Cullen. On 3 April 1857 Newman sent letters to Cullen and the Irish bishops telling them of his intention to resign. To Cullen he named St Laurence's Day, 14 November, as the day he would cease office: 'My most urgent reasons for this step are, the fatigue which I experience from my frequent passages between Dublin and Birmingham, the duty of the Rector to show himself in public more than my strength will allow, for the good of the University, and the need to my Congregation of my services which have been so long intermitted.'

The effect of Newman's decision was one of shock, and a number of people tried to persuade him to stay on and in turn persuade the Birmingham Oratorians to spare him for at least a year or two longer. Such was Dr Leahy's request as Vice-Rector, and it was echoed by many other influential people. In the summer of 1857 the three Irish Archbishops wrote to the Oratory asking if they could retain him as Rector 'as hitherto': they did not raise the question of non-residence. As Newman wrote to James Hope-Scott, 'It is now six years since I gave up my confessional, my weekly lecture, and my various internal duties; and the Congregation has been established little more than eight years, so that I have given to Dublin two thirds of the whole time, and the University has had the use of me far more than the Oratory.' As usual he feared most for the future of the Oratory: 'We do not oppose the continuance of my Rectorship, but my residence in Dublin. And I tell you fairly we shall fairly be wrecked here, if I am away longer. No novices will come, while I am away.'

The Irish hierarchy remained inactive. It was as though they could not believe Newman would actually retire. When he left for Birmingham on 19 November 1857 no successor had been appointed and no working Vice-Rector found. Much against their own wishes, the bishops found themselves with Newman continuing as a non-resident Rector. For the moment there was no other solution. It was not until 12 November 1858, after he had drawn up and presented a memorial requesting a proper Charter for the Catholic University, that Newman finally resigned. After that date he had no connection with the University which he had done so much for.

At the time the Catholic University venture did little to endear Newman to the Irish hierarchy of bishops, and served to augment a movement of feeling against him which was beginning to gather momentum in England and, through influence, at Rome. The years of the mid-fifties were certainly exacting for him, in command of two institutions, the Oratory and the University, writing copiously, sermons, the University Gazette, articles for the *Catholic Standard*, and in the summer of 1855 finishing off *Callista*, his second novel.

To add to his troubles Faber and his London Oratorians were unsettled, and dissatisfied with the nature of the two Oratory establishments. In October 1855, at a time when Newman had been a Catholic for ten years, he discovered that the London Oratorians had made application to the Congregation of Propaganda for an alteration of part of the Oratorian Rule in England. Cardinal Wiseman had asked Faber's help in undertaking the spiritual care and direction of some nuns. This particular task had been forbidden to the Oratories since the day of their founder, St

Philip Neri. Oratorians were supposed to devote their time to pastoral, educational and intellectual work, and they should not be diverted from it. The London Oratory applied for a suspension or adaptation of the Oratorian Rule which prohibited them from the spiritual care of nuns. Naturally enough, Propaganda thought that the application had Newman's approval, since he held the Pope's Brief for the Oratories in England. Newman knew nothing about it. Faber had not consulted him and he first learned of it from Dalgairns who, returning from the London Oratory on 16 October, showed him copies of the application to Propaganda. Dalgairns had been stopped by the Birmingham Oratory hearing the confession of nuns, and he had wished for a change in the Rule.

Propaganda consulted the London bishops, Wiseman and Grant, and Ullathorne, and prepared a dispensation from the Rule for the English Oratorians. Newman felt strongly that Faber should have consulted him, and that the Oratorian Rule, which was the basis and structure of the vocation which the Birmingham Oratorians had chosen, should not be changed for them unilaterally by another, quite distinct Oratorian House. This he pointed out to Faber in November and asked what he would have thought if the Birmingham House had pursued a similar course over some matter without the knowledge of London, which in the end would affect the vocation of the London Oratorians. He thought it not unreasonable, though, to petition Propaganda to recognize in some suitable way the principle that the Houses should be 'entirely independent of each other, and what one does is not the act of the other'. The letter was formal and subsequently it became clear that it had offended Faber: Newman thought that since he was the person who brought the English Rule of the Oratory to England all correspondence on such matters with Propaganda 'should be put in my hands to transmit to Rome'. The London Oratory declined to do this on the grounds that since their application had already gone forward, it would show disrespect to the Congregation of Propaganda to complicate the approach. In this way the open breach between the two Oratories was made and the correspondence and manoeuvrings which took place show ordinary human failings on both sides.

Newman decided that at the end of December 1855 he should go to Rome himself in order to sort out the muddle: he would not oppose the permissions being given to the London Oratory, but he would establish the clear independence of the two Houses. He went with St John and visited the North Italian Oratories on his way. Unknown to him at that time, circular letters from Faber and his Oratorians had arrived at his destinations before him and at the Congregation of Propaganda. He was made out to be personally ambitious and it was more than hinted that he wanted complete control, a generalate, over the English Oratories. Even though these charges were entirely ill-founded, they did not do Newman's reputation any good. Yet although the Prefect of the Congregation of Propaganda, Barnabo, mocked Newman, saying that he had run away from Dublin, he did re-emphasize Newman's original Brief, that it was for the whole of England, and added that any new Oratories would have to be founded through him.

None of this satisfied Faber and his friends and the summer of 1856 saw a heightening of tension, Stanton and Hutchinson going to Rome, and Dalgairns leaving the Birmingham Oratory to return to London. In spite of Barnabo's explanation that it was unnecessary to have a separate Brief for London, the two London Oratorians persisted, finally secured it, and made sure that there was a clause which prohibited the establishment of another Oratory in London. They knew that Newman had plans for one in the East End.

The extent of the bitterness felt between the two Houses is seen in a letter written by Faber to Stanton describing what Dalgairns had told him of Birmingham: 'The whole house, Bernard (Dalgairns) says, is extremely united in condemning us, in real spirits, not regretting the row, and considering themselves a very successful house and all that they could wish. He describes their feeling against us as something awful.' Dalgairns reported that J. S. Flanagan, one of Newman's Oratorians, had said that the London Oratory's 'professions of religion are simply "humbug".'

In mid-September Newman learned of the new Brief for London, and wrote ironically to St John, 'I had a letter from Talbot yesterday. He is acting with the London House. The new Brief is to floor us, by doing what *I* want and removing all complaint (without my sharing in the act) and then leading to the question, "Now *what* is the cause of complaint, what the grievance *now*? Why don't you make it up?' In October Newman was lamenting to St John, 'I go to Rome to be snubbed. I come to Dublin to be repelled by Dr McHale and worn away by Dr Cullen. The Cardinal taunts me with his Dedications, and Fr Faber insults me with his letters.' Newman felt himself the butt of all. The Cardinal was Wiseman who had wanted to dedicate his *Panegyric of St Philip Neri* to Newman and Faber jointly. Newman felt his name was being used to bolster the London Oratory and requested Wiseman that he should link his name with the Fathers of the Birmingham House. Wiseman was deeply offended and ignored the request: it was an incident which finally put Wiseman, who for such a long time had been kindly influential in Newman's fortunes, against him.

The split was achieved. Faber went his own way: Newman upheld the independence of the Birmingham institution, and, when he returned at last from the University, was able to devote his old care and attention to it.

Wiseman, already disaffected, was made to seem crossed again when Newman found himself embroiled in controversy over the liberal Catholic periodical the *Rambler*. Sir John Acton had acquired control of the *Rambler* both for political and intellectual reasons. He was to enter Parliament as a Whig and needed a journal in which he could put forward his views. He also wanted to air his theological ideas without the interfering domination of the Roman Catholic clergy. He ran into trouble when in the *Rambler* for August 1858 he described St Augustine as 'the father of Jansenism'. This term created resentment and an explanation, of which Acton disapproved, was published in September. He then persuaded his old tutor the theologian Johan Döllinger to write a letter on the subject. Wiseman found that Döllinger's letter was 'giving great pain and perhaps scandal' and thought the matter should be referred to an authority superior to his. Among those he consulted were Faber and Dalgairns who supported the idea: they thought that it was part of Wiseman's 'pastoral solicitude' to denounce the letter to the Holy See, because it was likely to lead the faithful into error.

On 1 January 1859 Acton wrote to the editor Richard Simpson describing his meeting with Newman at which the whole matter was discussed: 'I had a three hours' talk with the venerable Noggs who came out at last with his real sentiments to an extent which startled me, with respect both to things and persons, as H. E. [His Eminence], Ward, Dalgairns, etc., etc., natural inclination of men in power to tyrannise, ignorance and presumption of our would-be theologians, in short what you and I would comfortably say over a glass of whiskey.' Acton went on to say that the move was to break the *Rambler* and those who intended it showed jealousy of Döllinger, and that Newman 'inclined to the notion that the source is in Brompton'. Newman's advice was for Simpson to declare 'that we do not treat theology in our pages.' Newman's further advice to Acton showed that he was aware of a desired increase in power on the part of the English Ultramontanes, that is those who favoured the absolute authority of the Pope in matters of faith and discipline. He wrote saying that the *Rambler* should 'go back to its own literary line. Let it be instructive, clever and amusing. Let it cultivate a general temper of good humour and courtesy.' Yet he suggested as well, 'Let it adopt the policy of Wellington in the lines of Torres Vedras, who kept within shelter, while the enemy scoured the plain, but kept a sharp eye on him, and took him at disadvantage, whenever it was possible.'

The chief reason why the *Rambler* was disliked by Roman Catholic clergy was that it was carried on by laymen for laymen: the bishops especially distrusted it. Matters came to a head when the leading Catholic layman Scott Nasmyth Stokes criticized the English bishops for their handling of the question of state support for Catholic schools. The bishops were greatly displeased and at a meeting of some of them in London, they decided that unless Simpson resigned as editor, they would censure it in their pastoral letters. Simpson prudently resigned, but there was no successor. It became clear to all sides that Newman was the only acceptable person who might take on the task: he did so in order to save the educated laity, but only after much prayer and meditation.

His editorship was brief. He made it a bi-monthly magazine and published his first number in May 1859, making no criticism of his predecessors; in fact he continued it in much the same strain, valuing the part which the laity played in the life of the Church. The *Tablet* criticized it, pointing out that matters of faith were to be discussed as 'open questions' in the correspondence department. There would be no due homage to Catholic truth and no recognition of the just rights of ecclesiastical authority. Much later, in 1884, Newman wrote, 'I tried to make the old series of the Magazine in keeping with the new; and, when faults were objected to my first Number, I said, as to Mgr Manning, with a reference to the Great Eastern, which was then attempting to get down the river, that I too was striving to steer an unmanageable vessel through the shallows and narrows of the Thames, and that Catholic readers must be patient with me and give me time, if I was to succeed eventually in my undertaking.' No matter what his readers felt, the bishops were impatient. Ullathorne asked him, chiefly because of remarks about the laity in the *Rambler*, to give up the editorship. Newman quickly agreed but made it plain that it could only go back to Acton and Simpson because of the finance involved. Ullathorne accepted that this should happen after the July number.

Newman's farewell was to publish his own article 'On Consulting the Faithful in Matters of Doctrine'. It is ironical that a hundred years later the greater part of the teaching of this article is contained in the decrees of the second Vatican Council. At the time, it was received with indignation, and Bishop Brown of Newport secretly delated Newman's article to Rome for heresy.

Again, in this instance, conflicting personalities were to play their own parts which for a time acted against Newman's interests. Ullathorne gave the news of his delation to Propaganda early in 1860. Newman at once declared himself willing to explain everything in his article in a proper Roman Catholic sense. Wiseman accepted the role of intermediary between Newman and Propaganda whose Congregation prepared a list of questions for Newman to answer. In fact Wiseman never passed the list on, but sent Newman a message through Manning that he was not to worry and that he should be assured that Wiseman would settle the matter: like Döllinger's delation, it would not be proceeded with. Wiseman failed to explain to Rome what he was doing and for years Propaganda, principally Barnabo, thought that Newman had failed to comply with their demands. Consequently, in Rome, his reputation suffered; and in London too, where the Brompton Oratorians regarded him as no favourite and the Ultramontanes knew him to be a liberal and a supporter of the laity.

He disagreed with Manning, too, over the Pope's temporal power. In 1860 Pius IX was deprived of all his dominions except the Patrimony of St Peter. Most Catholics, even Acton and Döllinger, rallied to the Pope's cause. Newman thought that it was not essential for the Pope's spiritual authority for him to exercise temporal authority: he thought the Papacy would be better off without the latter. Those of similar views wanted him to speak out, in order to counter those on the other side, chief among whom was Manning. Newman refused and kept his silence which was interpreted once again by the Ultramontanes as disloyalty to the Pope.

Another issue brought him censure at this time as well, that of education. In May 1859 Newman had founded the Oratory School at Edgbaston; its first pupils being seven boys all the sons of converts: Father Nicholas Darnell became its Headmaster. It was to provide opportunities which the more notable Protestant Public Schools provided for other boys. It proved a great success and soon the sons of old, established Catholic families were being sent to it.

Much at the same time, Newman became interested in the plan to found a Catholic College at Oxford, although he did not intend to associate himself too closely with the project because of his connection with the Dublin University which he had founded at the Pope's wish. With the removal of religious tests in 1854, Catholics were beginning to go to Oxford. Manning and others were not enthusiastic about their mixing in Colleges or Universities with Protestants of any sort. Newman wished the scheme well but hoped that the Jesuits would take on the task. Complementary to this plan was one for building a new Catholic church in Oxford to commemorate the numerous conversions brought about by the Oxford Movement. Newman felt this move most unwise. It would be interpreted as an attack on the Church of England within its stronghold. He wrote to Edgar Estcourt, Ullathorne's secretary, that the controversial nature of any new church establishments in Oxford 'would be the very circumstance which would determine *me personally* against taking that part in promoting them, which you assign to me. It would do more harm than good.' He added, 'I have never acted in direct hostility to the Church of England. I have, in my lectures on Anglicanism, professed no more than

34. The Oratory School, Birmingham. Founded by Newman, the school is now at Woodcote in Oxfordshire

to carry on "the children of the movements of 1833" to their legitimate conclusions.' He ended by asserting that Ullathorne was 'against a convert having the Mission of Oxford: much more inexpedient would it be for a convert to take part in the erection of a new Church there.'

As it happened, his old Anglican friends gradually began to make contact with him again, and he with them. A touching letter from Isaac Williams recorded how God had granted him health to see another winter, and that the years were telling on John Keble. In reply, Newman wrote of his own physical condition, 'And I have been swilling cod liver oil up to ten days since. But all last year I fell off in flesh, and now I am an old man, and cannot get accustomed to the look of my fingers.' He marvelled that the age of death is so various: 'Some people live a second life – There is Robert Wilberforce dies at 54 – There is Lord Lyndhurst making speeches at 88. From 50 to 80 is as long as from 20 to 50.'

The year 1861 brought fresh troubles. He found himself being attacked by Protestants in a number of journals. He described his reaction to these gratuitous snipes at his integrity to Mary Du Boulay whom he had received into the Church in 1850. Most of them, he told her, were occasioned when *Essays and Reviews* came under censure from Establishment centres of power, such as the *Quarterly Review*. In the *Edinburgh Review*, he noted that A. P. Stanley wrote, '"Why, Dr Wilberforce is worse even than Dr Newman's Elucidations against Hampden," and then proceeds not to abuse Dr W but me.' He found all these attacks annoying:

35. This is one of the first photographs ever taken of Newman. He was photographed in London in December 1861 when he was on a visit to Mrs Bowden whose two sons later became priests of the London Oratory

'These are little and ridiculous things taken separately, but they form an atmosphere of *flies* – one can't enjoy a walk without this fidget on the nerves of the mind. They are nothing in the eye of reason, but they weary.'

Newman's greatest trial that year was over the Oratory School which Darnell had been running and turning more and more into a stereotype public school. At the same time there were rumours of complaint that the rule of silence was not observed by the boys in their dormitories and that there were other indisciplines. Darnell became jealous of his own authority and had to be reminded in mid-December 1861 that Newman was the Superior of the school and that it belonged to the Congregation. He told Darnell, 'If I wish to speak to the masters, dames etc I am not obliged to do so through you – nor need they speak to me thro' you. On the contrary there is ever an appeal to me from any of them, and a supervision on my part over all of them.' Matters came to a head when, just before Christmas, Darnell demanded complete control of the School, and, refusing any compromise, resigned with his staff. Newman was fired to act by the prospect of his school collapsing utterly and had to write around to his friends asking for recommendations for a new staff. He found his men, among whom was Thomas Arnold, junior, who had been Professor of English in Dublin, and Ambrose St John became the new Headmaster. James Hope-Scott and Edward Bellasis, an old convert friend, gave Newman great help, and the new term opened with a full complement of boys.

Again Newman's reputation was not improved by the incident. Darnell was the source of whispers against him, especially in London, and in any case the Oratory School was suspect because of the strong involvement of converts in it. Each cause he adopted, sometimes willingly, sometimes as a matter of duty, seemed to invite attack from the episcopate or more especially from the Ultramontanes. For the moment success eluded him. Even his proposed translation of the Vulgate version of the Bible foundered. In August 1857 Wiseman had asked him on behalf of the English Bishops to undertake a new translation. By December of the following year he was still awaiting firm instructions. He had spent a hundred pounds of his own money but Wiseman, because of the ill-feeling between the two Oratories, decided to delay the project and clearly preferred Newman not to be associated with it. There was also a great deal of hostility from booksellers and others who had vested interests in the sale of the Douai version.

Newman's reputation was at a remarkably low ebb in 1862. Never had it seemed that Church authority bore so heavily down on him.

Chapter 7 Recognition and esteem 1862–90

*'I write to express the joy we feel in your elevation to
the Sacred College.'* Cardinal Manning

The popular view was that Newman was dissatisfied with the Church of
his conversion. By June 1862 rumours had circulated that the liberal
Catholic, and defender of the laity's interests, was almost ready to cross
the divide back to the Church of England. Nothing was further from his
mind, but by 30 June he felt he had to repudiate the idea of his returning to
Anglicanism by publishing a letter in the *Globe*, then a leading Whig
organ. An ill-informed report had been printed a few days previously,
which alleged that he was about to leave the Oratory at Brompton as a
preliminary to returning to the Church of England. He put the *Globe* right
about his connection with Brompton and stressed, 'I have not had one
moment's wavering of trust in the Catholic Church ever since I was
received into her fold.' He added in especially vivid language that 'Protestantism is the dreariest of possible religions; that the thought of the
Anglican service makes one shiver, and the thought of the Thirty-nine
Articles makes me shudder. Return to the Church of England! no; "the net
is broken, and we are delivered." I should be a consummate fool (to use a
mild term) if in my old age I left "the land flowing with milk and honey"
for the city of confusion and the house of bondage.'

Later in the year Newman was called on by Ullathorne to condemn
both the *Rambler* and its successor, the *Home and Foreign Review*. This he did
without endorsing Ullathorne's criticisms, particularly of Simpson: it was
an act of canonical obedience on Newman's part. In fact he had been
pleased at the steady improvement of the *Home and Foreign Review*. When
he felt that people in general were associating himself with Ullathorne's
strictures, he made his position clear. Ullathorne had acted kindly and
wisely in associating Newman with his condemnation. As he wrote to
Newman, 'Your reputation is very dear to me, as to all good Catholics.
And I know how many persons both here and at Rome were uneasy in
consequence of the impressions which were industriously spread about
concerning a supposed sympathy on your part with the proceedings of Mr
Simpson and others.' Newman explained to him, 'In like manner, as I
should have withdrawn my own writings, had you condemned them with
such weight of authority, so I expressed to you in my letter my judgement,
that, since Mr Simpson's writings were so condemned, they also ought to
be withdrawn. Such a line of action on my part was prior to, and indepen-

36. W. B. Ullathorne, Newman's bishop at Birmingham

dent of, the question of the intrinsic truth or erroneousness of what he said. It was an act of *obedience*.' Acton closed the *Review*, which left the field clear to the Catholic periodicals controlled mainly by Ultramontanes and the London faction.

1863, despite rumour and accusations, saw Newman taking up old friendships with Anglicans. He met W. J. Copeland, who had been his curate at Littlemore, in London by chance, and Rogers paid him a visit in Birmingham. Keble, Williams and R. W. Church corresponded with him. In late summer Faber died: Newman attended his funeral in London.

At the very end of the year a severe blow was aimed at Newman. It was the culmination of troubles which had gathered over those past few years. He was sent anonymously, *MacMillan's Magazine* for January 1864, containing Charles Kingsley's review-article which impugned him. It later turned out that William Pope, a Yorkshire priest, had sent it him, 'Knowing how popular Mr Kingsley had become in Cambridge, and knowing, too, that MacMillan is very much read, especially by men at Oxford and Cambridge, I took the liberty of sending the shameful passage to you.' The passage read, apropos Queen Elizabeth I, 'Truth, for its own sake, had never been a virtue with the Roman clergy. Father Newman informs us that it need not, and on the whole ought not to be: that cunning is the weapon which Heaven has given to the saints wherewith to withstand the brute male force of the wicked world which marries and is given in marriage.' Newman wrote to MacMillan and Company, pointing out that the accusation was not backed up by evidence and that he wanted to draw their attention 'to a grave and gratuitous slander'. When it became clear by correspondence with Alexander MacMillan that Kingsley was indeed the author of the article, Newman expressed his astonishment, 'Had anyone said that it was Mr Kingsley, I should have laughed in his face. . . . I said to myself, "Here is a young scribe, who is making a cheap reputation by smart hits at safe objects".'

Kingsley was unable to prove his charge apart from referring in general terms to one of Newman's Anglican sermons, and offered an inadequate, equivocating apology. As Newman had informed Alexander MacMillan, 'Any letter addressed to me by Mr Kingsley, I account public property', and, urged by his friends, in February 1864 he published the correspondence on the affair with two pages of his own reflections, as a pamphlet which became known as *Mr Kingsley and Mr Newman*. His friends were delighted. He was advised to send copies to the London Clubs: copies went to the Athenaeum, the University Club, the Oxford and Cambridge, and the Catholic Stafford Club. It was a literary sensation. English Catholics, for a long time quietly sympathetic to Newman and his views, declared their support and saw him as their defender. An address of thanks for his staunch defence of Catholic integrity was presented to him by a hundred clergy of the Westminster diocese. Newman saw clearly that he had to be careful in acknowledgement for fear of offending the London Ultramontanes who held authority and power.

Kingsley retorted in March, publishing *What then does Dr Newman mean?* which was violent and biased in its charges. Newman wrote to Copeland on 31 March that, so far as he understood, the strength of what Kingsley said, to the popular mind, 'lies in the antecedent prejudice that *I was a Papist while I was an Anglican*. Mr K *implies this*. The only way in which I can destroy this is to give my history, and the history of my mind, from 1822 or earlier, down to 1845. I wish I had my papers properly about me.' This was exactly what he did, writing the *Apologia*. His friends rallied round, Catholic and Anglican alike, providing him with letters and checking facts. He had his own papers and letters organized only up to 1836. He had said to Jemima in 1863, 'When I have a little leisure, I recur to my pigeon-hole of letters, where they stand year by year from 1836 down to this date. I have digested them up to the former year. Thus I do a little work in the way of sifting, sorting, preserving, or burning.' Between 21 April and 2 June the *Apologia* came out each Thursday, and on 16 June he published an appendix. Almost a year later in May 1865 the definitive edition *History of My Religious Opinions* was published, a book of over five

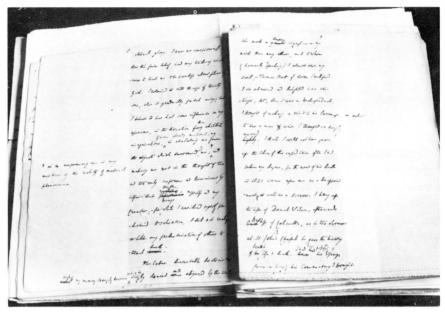

37. Manuscript of Newman's *Apologia*, 1864

hundred pages. He had made one or two alterations to answer the criticisms of Catholic friends. In deference to his friend David Moriarty, Bishop of Kerry, he changed remarks about the Church of England which some Catholics found offensive. Nevertheless when Charles Russell, President of Maynooth College, wanted him 'to withdraw the statement that the Pope in Ecumenical Council is the normal seat of Infallibility', and leave out 'that certain Italian devotions to our Lady are not suitable for England', Newman politely refused. He had found that he could use his arguments to defeat a Protestant attack on the Catholic Church for stating the moderate view in order to balance the extremist opinions of the Ultramontanes. Manning and Ward realized what he was doing and disliked it, but most English Catholics, and influential among them the old Catholics, appreciated what he was doing and supported him. The *Apologia* was a notable success: Newman's influence was never greater. Not only was he popular at home, he became popular abroad. The Birmingham Oratory had never been so sought out by people wanting to meet him.

Even so those in authority still thwarted him. Ullathorne had for some time been wanting a mission at Oxford, which was in the Birmingham diocese, and offered it to Newman in August 1864. Newman bought a five-acre site where a workhouse had once stood, now Wellington Square, and Ullathorne encouraged him to start collecting money for a church there. Manning and other Ultramontane converts thought any form of

Oxford education for Roman Catholics was dangerous, and Newman's influence in Oxford they regarded as potentially even more dangerous. Persuading Wiseman to his views, they secured the intervention of Propaganda in Rome, which called a meeting of the English bishops. Propaganda formally disapproved of Catholics attending Protestant universities and in March 1865 the English bishops declared that parents should not send their sons to Protestant universities and that Catholic Colleges should not be established in them. Newman, and many powerful lay-members, disagreed, but he nevertheless in disappointment sold the Oxford site. Early in 1865 Wiseman died, and in June Manning was consecrated as Archbishop of Westminster in his place.

Manning had written to Newman asking him to attend the ceremony at Moorfields. Newman accepted, taking the opportunity to hope that Manning would not now do his best to have him made a bishop 'in partibus'. Manning assured him that for more than two years he had tried to accomplish Newman's elevation. He saw the position not as decoration, but as having a fitness about it for someone of Newman's standing. Newman emphasized he would persistently decline the honour.

Manning's power was at its zenith. He was now Archbishop in succession to Wiseman and Ward was editor of the *Dublin Review* which he made the chief organ of extremist, ultramontane views. Newman stayed with the Anglican, Frederic Rogers, when in London for the consecration and did not attend Manning's celebratory banquet. Manning was offended at Newman's failing the banquet, and his old suspicions were aroused. Newman saw plainly that there was no chance of an Oxford establishment for the Church in the near future.

Rogers and Church made him happy though, by telling him to buy a violin at their expense. He wrote to Rogers on 25 June, 'I have chosen a violin – and, in choosing it, have gone merely by what seemed to be its easiness for my fingers ... I thank you and Church for it very much.' His old friends supported him in many ways, and his violin was a great consolation to him from first to last.

In the public eye his popularity was further increased by the publication of *The Dream of Gerontius*, which appeared in the magazine the *Month*. Its success, which surprised Newman, made him collect his poetry in one volume which, too, was widely bought and went into many editions.

Increasingly Newman found that he could exert considerable influence through his writings: he could espouse a moderate interpretation of doctrine in face of the open hostility of Ultramontane Catholics, namely Manning and Ward. The business of trying to found an Oxford Oratory showed the political manoeuvrings which went on. Pusey, whom Newman was to meet in September of 1865 at Keble's Hursley vicarage, wrote a critical reply to Manning's *Workings of the Holy Spirit in the Church of England, a Letter to the Rev. E. B. Pusey*: he entitled it *An Eirenicon in a Letter to the Author of 'The Christian Year'*, and attacked Catholic doctrine and devotion concerning the Virgin Mary, and the infallibility claimed for the Papacy. Newman in turn was critical of Pusey largely because he gave the impression that Manning's ultramontane views were those acceptable to English Catholics. He wrote his *Letter to the Rev. E. B. Pusey* in November and December 1865 stating moderate Catholic views which were widely held and represented traditional teaching. He worked at this letter in most trying circumstances when extremely ill with 'the stone'. He could not understand his illness: he languished through December and into January. His diary entry for 8 January asked 'What is the matter with me?' To Rogers he wrote, 'Till Sunday last I have been all day in bed. For thirty years I have not had so anxious an illness.' He would not go out for fear of having a painful attack 'in a railway carriage, or at a friend's house.' He said, 'The doctor puts it down to the fidget caused by the letter I have written to Pusey – but though any application of mind tries me, I cannot credit him.' On 17 January he entered in his diary, '$\frac{1}{2}$ past 2 A.M. got rid of the unsuspected *causa mali*.'

The Letter to Pusey was published on 31 January 1866 and was meant to be a real means to unity. He showed his clear preference for 'English habits of devotion to foreign', and rejected innovations and exaggerations introduced by Faber and Ward particularly. At once many old Catholics, priests and laymen, rallied to him.

In the meantime Ullathorne had again asked Newman to take the Oxford mission and found an Oratory there. Manning was naturally unsympathetic to Newman having any contact with Oxford. *The Letter to Pusey* was to prove it. Talbot revealed his fears writing to Manning, 'I am afraid that the *Home and Foreign Review* and the old school of Catholics will rally round Newman in opposition to you and Rome.' Manning saw great danger in Newman's type of English Catholicism, 'It is the old Anglican, patristic, literary, Oxford tone transplanted into the Church.' His opposition to Newman was wholehearted but not open which Newman did not relish. Not only was he opposed by powerful forces at home, he was undermined in Rome: Talbot saw to that.

Both Ward and Manning wanted a highly critical and censorious article on Newman's views printed in the *Dublin Review*, but neither Ullathorne nor Bishop Clifford of Clifton would revise it: the device, aimed at publishing episcopal disapproval of Newman, was abandoned.

At the end of March 1866 Ullathorne saw his opportunity again for persuading Newman to undertake the Oxford venture. Manning's desire to make Newman unacceptable for appointment in Oxford by censure in

38. H. E. Manning, once Archdeacon of
Chichester, who succeeded Wiseman as
Cardinal Archbishop of Westminster in 1865

the *Dublin Review* had failed. Newman insisted that his Mission and the
establishment of an Oratory should be approved and guaranteed by
Propaganda. As he wrote to Ullathorne, he was in fact 'indifferent how the
Holy See in its wisdom decides': he undertook 'the mission of Oxford with
"reluctance"'. He wanted the Oxford House to be an integral part of the
Birmingham Oratory during his lifetime and thought it should remain so
at least three years after his death. In the end, after a year of many
vicissitudes, Keble's death, Gerard Manley Hopkins's reception into the
Church at Birmingham Oratory, among them, Propaganda gave permission that an Oratory should be built at Oxford dependent on that of
Birmingham. Ullathorne wrote the news to him on Christmas Day. It was
not until the following April 1867 that the full text of the permission
became known to Newman: Ullathorne omitted an important part which
instructed him to call Newman back from Oxford 'blande suaviterque',
courteously and gently, if he went there himself.

Ullathorne's admission of the 'secret Instruction', prompted Newman
to tell St John that had he known of it, he would 'not have entered into any
engagement to take the Mission'. The statement was occasioned by a
'public insult in the *Weekly Register*'. Its Rome correspondent, E. R.
Martin, had reported that Propaganda had not given permission for
Newman to reside in Oxford on instruction from the Pope. Confidence

39. An engraving of 'Father Newman' in 1866

was lacking in him because of his recent writings: 'Only an Ultramontane without a taint in his fidelity could enter such an arena as that of Oxford life with results to the advantage of the faith in England.' The influential Catholic laity again rallied to Newman and published an address to him in the *Tablet*: William Monsell MP collected five hundred signatures which included the Deputy Earl Marshal, Lord Howard, Viscount Norreys, Lord Henry Kerr, many MPs, several judges, and the rest all prominent names in one way or another. Ranged against Newman was the dominant party, Manning, Talbot, Manning's disciple Herbert Vaughan in Rome, Ward, and the chief periodicals.

Barnabo's ear was poisoned. He had reprimanded Newman about the Oratory School accusing him of training boys for future education at Oxford. Newman stoutly defended himself. His distrust of Manning grew. Earlier in the year when Ullathorne told him that Manning was going to visit Birmingham and that a meeting might be advisable, Newman replied that he would, but that 'I will say to your Lordship frankly, that I cannot trust the Archbishop. It seems to me he never wishes to see a man except for his own ends ... Certainly I have no wish to see him now; first because I don't like to be practised on; secondly because I cannot in conversation use smooth words which conceal, not express thoughts; thirdly because I am not sorry he should know that I am dissatisfied with him.'

40. The Oratory retreat house at Rednal near Birmingham, during an outing of the Brothers of the Little Oratory

Newman was not put off by Ultramontane attacks, and at least in the end, Barnabo and Propaganda were put right about him. In April 1867 he allowed one of his Oratorians, Ignatius Ryder, to publish a pamphlet attacking Ward for his extreme views on Papal infallibility, and a little later in Rome, St John was able to lift a little the cloud which Newman was under. He managed to reveal to Propaganda that Newman was not disobedient in failing to answer the questions which had been put to him over the delated article 'On Consulting the Faithful in Matters of Doctrine.' The fault had lain with Manning and Ward who had promised to settle the affair satisfactorily without his answers, but who had kept silent.

Manning and Newman corresponded from the end of July through to the beginning of September about their differences and estrangement. Newman finally wrote to him on 2 September in this tone, 'I do not think your new conclusion will bear examination better than your old one', and, 'For my own part, I consider the world judges of the present by the present, and not by the past. I write this as a protest, and an appeal to posterity.' Nevertheless, as most usual, he added his purpose 'to say seven Masses' for the Archbishop's intentions. Naturally enough Manning found Newman 'very difficult' and the series of letters most unsatisfactory.

During August Newman formally resigned the Oxford Mission. So far as Propaganda was concerned the matter was at an end. Newman had the trouble of explaining the decision to the many subscribers to an Oxford Oratory: most asked him to use their donations for some other purpose.

He had also to explain the Church's position on university education to parents of the boys at his school. The English bishops decided to forbid Catholics from attending Protestant universities. On 20 October Ullathorne's pastoral on this subject was read out in diocesan churches. The ban continued until three years after Manning's death.

The years 1868 and 1869 were spent partly in eclipse. Approaches were made to Newman for him to attend the coming first Vatican Council, one invitation coming from Bishop Dupanloup, a French educationalist and Bishop of Orleans, to go as his theologian. He declined politely. Age and discomfiture in committees made him reluctant: he said that on boards and committees 'I have always felt out of place and my words unreal'. Much of his time was spent in the composition of *A Grammar of Assent*, mostly at Rednal. He wanted to show how reasonable it was for people to have certitude, and especially certitude in religion. He confessed that there is no such thing as a perfect logical demonstration, 'there is always a margin of objection – even in mathematics, except in the case of short proofs, as the propositions of Euclid. Yet on the other hand it is a paradox to say there is not such a state of mind as certitude.'

Manning bothered him again. The Archbishop had excommunicated Edmund Ffoulkes for a pamphlet he had written called *The Church's Creed or the Crown's Creed*. In the conflict it had been rumoured that Manning had withheld Newman's letter of explanation to Rome after the *Rambler* delation. Newman's reply through Ullathorne was curt, 'I know nothing, and never have had, nor have, nor can have, the slightest suspicion, of Dr Manning ever at any time having suppressed any letter of mine written to Cardinal Wiseman, and containing matter which had an ulterior destination.' Manning was by no means satisfied and wrote directly to Newman. Again Newman's response was clipped and immediate, 'I can only repeat what I said when you last heard from me. I do not know whether I am on my head or my heels when I have relations with you. In spite of my friendly feelings, this is the judgment of my intellect.'

In this state of affairs Newman set about finishing *A Grammar of Assent* published in March of the following year, and Manning at the head of English Ultramontanes set out for the Council, which opened on 8 December 1869. Newman's chief worry about the Council was that it would become concerned with the issue of Papal Infallibility. He knew that the Ultramontanes, the infallibilists, would seek a definition at the Council. He saw no need for one: 'What heresy calls for a decision?' he wrote to David Moriarty. He pointed out that 'the fears of some unknown definition, when everything is at rest, is secretly distressing numbers ...

The frogs said to the boys who threw stones at them "It is fun to you, but death to us." Where is the Arius or Nestorious, whose heresy makes it imperative for the Holy Church to speak?'

So strongly did he feel that he sent a confidential letter to Bishop Ullathorne protesting at the Ultramontane faction; and since it was a private letter, it was strongly worded. He accused the extremists of causing troubles and complications, and unrest among the laity, when there was no need for it: all held the Holy Father to be infallible: definition was not required. Was such occupation the proper work for an Ecumenical Council? He asked, 'Why should an aggressive insolent faction be allowed to "make the heart of the just to mourn, whom the Lord hath not made sorrowful?" Why can't we be let alone, when we have pursued peace, and thought no evil?' He went on to make it clear that many of the faithful were 'angry with the Holy See for listening to the flattery of a clique of Jesuits, Redemptorists and converts'. All might have been well, but Ullathorne showed the letter to a number of people in Rome, and among them Bishop Clifford of Clifton took a copy. By the middle of February an accurate transcript was in the hands of the Foreign Secretary, the Earl of Clarendon, and Acton had sent a copy to Döllinger. Soon unofficial versions were about, and finally Newman had to publish the authoritative text in the *Standard*. It made his position publicly known and he hoped his views might restrain the extremists. Despite all, the definition was laid down that when the Pope speaks *ex cathedra*, as shepherd and teacher of all Christians, and lays down truth concerning faith and morals, he enjoys protection from error, and needs no subsequent ratification of his definitions.

It was not that Newman failed to believe this doctrine: he simply found that its prosecution at the Council disturbed the faith of so many. Now he urged acceptance. He wrote to Anna Whitty, a convert and wife of the founder of the *Liverpool Daily Post*,'For three hundred years at least the Church has *acted* on the belief that the Pope was infallible *ex cathedra*, and no great harm has come of it; I trust that (in spite of a theological opinion having become dogma) the future will not differ from the past.' Again he made his usual point about general acceptance by the Church being, 'the ultimate guarantee of revealed truth.' Securus judicat orbis terrarum. How could Almighty God, 'allow 530 bishops to go wrong?'

While the Council had been busy with spiritual matters, temporal powers had once again come into direct conflict: on 19th July the Franco–Prussian war began. By September Rome was in the hands of Victor Emmanuel. As he wrote to Monsell at the end of the year, 'The definition of July involved the dethronement of September.' With historical foresight, Newman approved the limitation of the Pope's worldly

41. An 'Oxford' caricature with the High Anglican St Barnabas' Church, Oxford, in the background: Newman and Manning stand in the foreground.

power: he considered it would make the Papacy more universally acceptable spiritually; and he looked forward to the time when the Papacy would be open to men of all nations.

Very soon a direct challenge was made in England to the doctrine of Papal Infallibility. *The Times* in its second leader of 6 September 1872 maintained that the Popes had never disowned responsibility for the Massacre of St Bartholomew's Day, and now that Popes were infallible, it would be more than ever impossible for them to do so. It went on to ask, 'who disavows the deed? No Catholic does, so far as we know; at least, nobody whose authority, as entitled to speak for his Church, can be introduced into this question.' And nobody did: no one in authority stepped forward. Newman received a letter beseeching him to answer the leader, and finally in default of any other Catholic reply, he made the position clear. As he wrote, 'I have no claim to speak for my brethren; but I speak in default of better men.' He was unequivocal, 'No Pope can make evil good. No Pope has any power over those eternal moral principles which God has imprinted on our hearts and consciences.' He mentioned questions of fact which historians had to decide, and if Gregory XIII had a share in the guilt, then 'his infallibility is in no respect compromised. Infallibility is not impeccability. Even Caiaphas prophesied; and Gregory XIII was not quite a Caiaphas.'

There were other preoccupations, too, for Newman, besides this

42. The latest Vatican Decree – 'William kiss my toe!' Left to right: Döllinger, Gladstone, Thomas Capel (Rector of the short-lived Catholic University College, Kensington), Pius IX, Manning, Newman

theological debate. His efforts on behalf of the Oratory School did not diminish in these early years of the seventies, even though he was busy enough republishing his work in a uniform edition. A chapel was built for the school and land next to the school bought for playing fields. After ten years as its Prefect, St John was able to retire and handed on the task to the new headmaster, John Norris, who held the position until 1911.

There were various plans to found an English Catholic University, but none of the schemes attracted Newman. Manning's proposal for a University College at Kensington aroused his distrust: he felt its academic independence would suffer too much at the hands of its clerical masters. Towards the end of 1873 he was asked to be a member of its Senate and so to assume some responsibility for it. Added to the fact that at 72 he did not feel able to travel often to London, there was the discovery in the prospectus that Manning wanted it connected in a special way to London University. He had always regarded London University, as he informed Manning, as 'a body which has been the beginning and source, and symbol of all the Liberalism existing in the educated classes for the last forty years'. The Kensington University College opened without him in 1875 and closed as a failure in 1878.

Juvenal's tenth *Satire* reminds its readers that the reward of long life is to

suffer the deaths of one's friends. In 1873 Newman saw many of his closest
companions depart, Edward Bellasis, Henry Wilberforce, James Hope-
Scott, John Walker, and his doctor, George Evans. He wrote to John
Hungerford Pollen on 23 July, 'What a strange number of deaths of
friends has marked this year! at least to me. Sam Wilberforce is the last – I
call him Sam, because it recalls old days. I never knew him well, but I
have before me quite clearly the vision of his coming up to residence at
Oriel in 1823, leaning on Robert's arm. Ah me, what an age ago! it is a new
world; yet to the great Creator of all worlds it is but yesterday.'

The years 1874 and 1875 were largely occupied by controversy with
Gladstone, whose Irish University Bill had been defeated in Parliament.
Gladstone saw treachery afoot in the land, especially among those who
seemed to owe their allegiance first to the Pope rather than to England. In
the *Contemporary Review* he wrote that 'No one can be her (Rome's) convert
without renouncing his moral and mental freedom and placing his civil
loyalty and duty at the mercy of another.' He followed this up by publishing a popular pamphlet *The Vatican Decrees in their bearing on Civil Allegiance:
a Political Expostulation.* By the end of 1874, 150,000 copies had been sold.
Newman realized that it was his duty to answer Gladstone on behalf of
converts, many of whom he was responsible for attracting to the Catholic
Church; and many friends urged him to the defence. Bishop Brown asked
Newman 'to become our David against the Goliath who threatens us all',
Ambrose Phillipps de Lisle wrote, 'If anyone is to repel the shock, I think
you and you alone are the Man.' Lord Emly, formerly William Monsell,
M.P., begged him not to leave 'Ward and Co to represent the English
Catholics.' Lady Fullerton, an 1846 convert, thought Newman alone
'could meet the sophistry of Gladstone's genius with superior genius to his
and the calm reasoning which the task requires': there was no one with
'greater powers of mind and language.'

At the age of seventy-three he accepted his task, but at first found it
difficult making many false starts, so diffuse were Gladstone's arguments.
At last on 24 November he recorded in his diary, '(plucking every morning
what I had done the day before) till today, when I suddenly began my first
section (Introductory Remarks),' and he decided ingeniously to make his
reply to Gladstone a pamphlet in the form of *A Letter to the Duke of Norfolk.*
The Duke had been educated at the Oratory School, was a friend, and an
important Catholic layman: he was a notable Englishman, an obvious
victim of Gladstone's attack.

Newman at once emphasized in *A Letter* that the Ultramontane extremists were responsible for Gladstone's misunderstanding of the Catholic
position: they had been 'conducting themselves as if no responsibility
attached to wild words and overbearing deeds'. They were the ones, 'who

43. Father Ambrose St John, Newman's closest friend during his Roman Catholic days. They share the same grave at Rednal

at length having done their best to set the house on fire, leave to others the task of putting out the flame.' He analysed Gladstone's arguments and insisted that he was objecting not to the Pope but to a Church: 'It is the powers themselves and not their distribution that he writes against.' The claims of sovereignty whether made by Church or State, Newman declared, have their limitations: in the end, individual conscience is supreme. This did not imply a freedom to do as one pleased. It was above all an obedience to God: if in an extreme case, the Pope made laws or gave orders which were immoral, he was not to be obeyed. He argued that his views on the supremacy of conscience were those of the Catholic Church: the second Vatican Council has removed all doubt.

A Letter was received with wide acclaim and with relief, and generally recognized to be a brilliant riposte to Gladstone's thrust. David Moriarty wrote from Kerry, 'Many thanks for the coup de grace you have given to the faction who would allow none to be Catholics but Dublin Reviewers and Tablet Editors.' Approval came to him from all sides, Jesuits, old Catholics from the north of England, and seminary professors. Naturally, the extremists saw to it that complaints were made at Rome, but Manning was prudent enough to realize that serious harm would be done to English Catholicism if there were any hint of public censure from the hierarchy.

Personal relations between Gladstone and Newman were considerate, polite and friendly, showing the respect in which each held the other. Gladstone thanked Newman 'for the genial and gentle manner in which

44. A 'Spy' cartoon of Newman from
Vanity Fair, January 1877

you have treated me', and commented, 'Your spirit has been able to invest even these painful subjects with something of a golden glow.'

Sadly, a few months later Ambrose St John fell ill. He died towards the end of May. Newman was grief-stricken at the loss of his friend of thirty-two years' standing. Newman had expected the younger man to outlive him and become his literary executor. He wrote that 'Ambrose died of overwork . . . the translation of Fessler from the German was the last load upon the camel's back'. St John had produced the English translation of Fessler's *True and False Infallibility* in January 1875 which had supported Newman's defence against Gladstone. Newman wrote a long and moving account of St John's death to Emily Bowles, one of his most frequent correspondents, and months after he wrote to Mary Holmes, a convert of 1844, 'I do not expect ever to get over the loss I have had. It is an open wound, which in old men cannot be healed.'

St John's death was a desperate blow to the old man, but with his usual dedication Newman applied himself to his usual routine, preaching, examining the Oratory School boys, receiving visitors, among them Gladstone, Wilfrid Scawen Blunt, and Thomas Arnold who was taken back into the Church. He spent much time in re-editing his former works, *The Via Media of the Anglican Church* which had previously been called *Lectures on the Prophetical Office of the Church*, *An Essay on the Development of Christian Doctrine*, and he began preparing for publication *Select Treatises of St. Athanasius*.

Throughout the years 1874 to 1878, Newman from time to time sat for his portrait, first by Lady Coleridge and latterly by W. W. Ouless, who painted two pictures, one for Birmingham Oratory and the other for Oriel College.

The most significant event of 1877 for Newman was the invitation of S. W. Wayte, President of Trinity College, Oxford, to accept the position of an Honorary Fellow. Wayte's note was brief, finishing up, 'I may mention that if you should do so, you will be the first person in whose case the College will have exercised the power which was given to it in 1857, and that at present it is not contemplated to elect another Honorary Fellow.' Newman immediately replied that he was extremely honoured but that he would have to reflect before accepting. Such was the reputation of Newman now, that even his old Oxford College wanted to acknowledge him. He consulted Ullathorne who gave him warm support: '. . . I cannot see what objection can in any propriety be raised to your frankly responding to an act of courtesy and kindness which involves nothing whatsoever beyond a renewal of good feeling between your old College and yourself. I look upon it as a social good which, if God wills, may not be the only good.' Reassured, just before Christmas he wrote to Wayte his grateful thanks, accepting 'with a full heart an honour which is as great a surprise to me as it is a pleasure'. Dean Church commented, 'And to think that Oriel should have missed doing it first.'

Oxford was still officially banned to English Catholics, but Newman's honour was a major signal raised towards integration, or 'mixing', in education against which the Ultramontane Catholics continued to stand firm. At the end of February 1878 he went to Oxford as Wayte's guest. H. P. Liddon, Pusey's biographer, reported that he met him at dinner in Trinity: Newman talked briskly and was 'greatly pleased at the occasion of his return to Oxford'.

Newman wrote to Mrs William Froude that everyone at Trinity was 'abundantly kind' and informed her, 'I saw there my old Tutor, Short, in the same Rooms in which he had encouraged and rowed me as an undergraduate, in which he had been my opportune bottle holder when I was standing at Oriel and much discouraged. That was 58 years ago. He is now almost blind and could not see me. He is 87 and has three Oxford friends older than himself.' He called on Pusey, looked over the new Keble College, and visited Oriel.

Just prior to his restitution at Oxford, Pope Pius IX had died, on 7 February: on the 20th, Leo XIII was elected Pope. Later in that year, while the Birmingham Oratory was enjoying revival through new novices, two leading Catholic laymen, Edward Howard, the Duke of Norfolk, and the Marquis of Ripon, proposed that the Holy See should honour Newman by making him a Cardinal. Their first moves were made through Manning: they sought it not only as recognition for Newman himself but also as a public approval of his work and of his account of the Catholic Church and its teaching. Naturally, Manning was not over-enthusiastic, but complied by sending a letter through Cardinal Howard to the Pope. It had not arrived my mid-December 1878, and the first approach was made by Norfolk in an audience with Leo XIII at the beginning of that month.

At the end of January 1879, the Cardinal Secretary of State, Nina, enquired through Manning and Ullathorne whether or not Newman would accept the Cardinal's hat. Newman conferred with Ullathorne, in the end welcoming the offer as a recognition of his work, but hoping that the Pope would allow him to stay at the Oratory, and not reside in Rome. Ullathorne wrote to Manning officially stating that residence was the only difficulty, and enclosing Newman's official letter to himself, expressing concern about the Oratory. Newman's letter was intensely moving, begging permission to stay at Birmingham: 'I pray and entreat his Holiness in compassion of my diffidence of mind, in consideration of my feeble health, my nearly eighty years, the retired course of my life from my youth, my ignorance of foreign languages, and my lack of experience in business, to let me die where I have so long lived. Since I know now and henceforth that his Holiness thinks kindly of me, what more can I desire.'

The following six weeks turned into a time of anguish through a series of misunderstandings largely brought about by Manning's management. There must exist more than just a suspicion that he acted unsympathetically, deviously and politically in the affair. On 4 February he sent forward Newman's letter to Nina, but held back Ullathorne's urging that Newman should be allowed to stay at the Oratory. Ullathorne was suspicious of Manning and realized that Newman's letter might be interpreted as a refusal, and wrote to Manning again. Manning wasted no time in letting it be known in London that Newman had declined the Cardinalate: in addition, en route from Rome, he wrote to Norfolk informing him of the refusal. Ullathorne by now was roused, and sent a copy of his letter to Manning, direct to Cardinal Nina. On 18 February *The Times* announced that the offer had been made by the Pope, and had been refused. Two days later Newman wrote to Norfolk not to believe false reports. No statement, he pointed out, could have come from him: the affair was confidential: 'Nor could it come from Rome, for it was made public before my answer got to Rome – It could only come then from someone who, not only read my letter, but instead of leaving the Pope to interpret it, took upon himself to put an interpretation upon it, and published that interpretation to the world.'

Punch printed a jingle and showed no respect for Manning:

A Cardinal's Hat! Fancy NEWMAN in *that*,
    For the crown o'er his grey temples spread!
'Tis the good and great head that would honour the hat,
    Not the hat that would honour the head.

There's many a priest craves it: no wonder *he* waives it,
    Or that we, the soiled head-covering scanning,
Exclaim with one breath, *sans* distinction of faith
    'Would they wish NEWMAN ranked with OLD MANNING?'

Manning was obviously implicated, and Norfolk wrote to him enclosing a copy of the letter he had received from Newman. The result was that Manning quickly explained to the Pope that he had misunderstood Newman's original letter: he had not turned down the Cardinalate. Leo XIII at once responded by saying that Newman's elevation would not necessitate his leaving the Oratory. Lord Selborne's daughter reported the Pope's reaction when she and her father delivered a message to the Pope in

45. Newman, second from left in front row, and a group of fellow Oratorians

1887: 'My Cardinal! it was not easy, it was not easy. They said he was too liberal, but I had determined to honour the Church in honouring Newman. I always had a cult for him. I am proud that I was able to honour such a man.' So the matter was settled, but, yet again, not without much trouble created by the interference of the Cardinal Archbishop.

On 27 February Newman's mind was set at rest by a telegram sent to Ullathorne by Manning saying that 'Dr Newman will receive letters as desired;' and, in order that there should be no possibility of a new misunderstanding, Ullathorne himself backed up Newman's acceptance by a letter to Manning:

> The whole press of England has been engaged on the subject and the general disposition is to look upon Dr Newman not merely as a Catholic but as a great Englishman, and to regard the intention of the Pope as an honour to England.
>
> Your communication came happily in time to stop the general conclusion that Dr Newman had declined, upon which the comic papers had founded their illustrations.
>
> I have considered it prudent, now that all is public, to deny, and cause it to be denied, that Dr Newman has or did decline . . .

On 18 March Cardinal Nina's official letter announcing Newman's Cardinalate arrived in Birmingham. There followed many addresses of congratulation, and a month later he travelled to Rome to have his first audience with Leo XIII. He was received with great affection. Ullathorne had told how the deaths of St John and Edward Caswall, another long-serving Oratorian, had particularly affected Newman, 'He can never refer to these losses without weeping and becoming speechless for a time': now, when the Pope asked after the community of the Oratory, and Newman replied that they had lost some, Leo XIII placed his hand on his head and said, 'Don't cry.'

His impressions of Leo XIII are preserved in a letter to Henry Bittleston, a friend and Oratorian. The Pope asked him expected questions about the Oratory and where he studied theology, and Newman gave him the Roman edition of his four Latin Dissertations. He observed, 'I certainly did not think his mouth large till he smiled, and then the ends turned up, but not unpleasantly – he has a clear white complexion his eyes somewhat bloodshot – but this might have been the accident of the day. He speaks very slowly and clearly and with an Italian manner.'

Newman was recognized as a great man. He was treated like a statesman. The *Guardian* reported that what he said passed 'verbatim, along the telegraph wires like the words of the men who sway the world'. He took as his titular church in Rome, San Giorgio in Velabro. Later he was given a picture of it. Anne Pollen, a daughter of John Hungerford Pollen, recorded in her diary Newman's story of how he acquired it:

46. Newman in his Cardinal's robes, photographed in Rome, 1879. The tall figure behind Newman is Father William Neville who looked after him in his last years

He showed us a pretty old water-colour painting of St Giorgio in Velabro, his church in Rome. He said – 'I came by it in a very curious way: on my way back from Rome, after I was made Cardinal, I stayed a night in the country, at the house of a protestant clergyman, an old friend. He said to me – "Look at this curious picture of the Rienzi Palace." I looked at it, and said at once – "O that is St Giorgio in Velabrum" whereupon my friend said – "Then I must give it you," and took it off his wall, and I took it on with me to Birmingham.'

Preparing for that return he wrote to Father John Norris about his accommodation at the Oratory:

It is useless to think of preparing *my* rooms. Two days before I return they may be swept out – but I must ask the Fathers to let me rent the one next to my own, (Number ii) and I must have an altar there. Then I must have endless wardrobes for my vestments, and for robes, which I shall never wear. I almost think I shall be dead before I am to rights. My tailor's bill will be £200! And, when I am gone, nothing will be of use to any one, unless indeed some articles may cut up into chasubles and veils.

47. Newman's room at the Birmingham Oratory. (The lamp was given to him by
Gladstone.)

48. The chapel in Newman's room. Over the altar (to the left of the picture) is a portrait
of St Francis de Sales, patron of writers, but the pictures on the wall largely depict some
of Newman's younger friends who followed him into the Roman Catholic Church. On
the left is Henry Wilberforce, son of Samuel Wilberforce

After illness in Rome, and a relapse in Leghorn, he was back in Birmingham by July, and at the end of the year he was presented with a carriage by Lord Coleridge, Lord Blachford, W. J. Copeland and Dean Church, 'The brougham came all right yesterday, and is the admiration of all who have seen it.' He was amused by his acting coachman praising it for being in such good taste. The one great sadness of that Christmas was his sister Jemima dying on Christmas Day itself at the age of seventy-two.

Newman's own health was in decline. Old age made recovery difficult. In January 1880 he fell in his room and broke a rib. Anne Pollen wrote in her diary that he could not be visited for about a week: 'We hope and pray for him to get better – at his age of course, there is cause for anxiety – dear old man.' The next month he fell again, and broke two more ribs.

Yet he recovered, and at seventy-nine continued preaching, writing, and visiting. He stayed with Norfolk in London and in May 1880 preached both in the morning and in the evening at St Aloysius' Church in Oxford. Anne Pollen told how her father one day saw Newman alone: 'He was low about his health, and kept saying that he was 79. "My dear Cardinal," says F, "do you forget that Blücher won the battle of Waterloo at 85?" "Yes," said the Cardinal with a smile, "and Radetsky was 92".' That autumn he spent a great deal of time working on *Select Treatises of St. Athanasius*. In February of the following year it was published.

Age was now having its effect: his fingers stiffened, making it difficult and painful to write: his letters were briefer than before. He still preached whenever he could, and took the opportunity of doing so at the London Oratory, when he was staying there in the summer of 1881 in order to have his portrait painted by John Millais. He pointed out to Father William Gordon at Brompton the difficulties of promising at his age to preach: 'I cannot reckon on my strength, and, when that goes, my head goes, and I am fit for nothing but to come down the pulpit steps. And then it is a continual tease to me that people are *looking forward* to my preaching, and brings about the very incapacity which I fear.' His sermon was short: Anne Pollen wrote that it concerned 'the importance of religious education for the young, and the fallacy of those who pretended that secular and religious education could be distinct one from the other . . . The Cardinal was looking very well and comparatively strong.'

In her words the Millais portrait was 'becoming a splendid thing'. Newman sat for the painting in the artist's studio most days. Anne Pollen noted, 'The Cardinal having called Millais Apelles, he now goes by that name. Apelles' manners, Fr Stanton says, are remarkable; he calls Newman Mr Cardinal, and talks to him with his pipe in his mouth. These proceedings with a man of the Cardinal's age and distinction are certainly

49. Portrait of Cardinal Newman by Millais, 1881

in the worst of taste. But the portrait is the important thing, and Millais is enchanted with the Cardinal's head and is very keen on painting it. He has offered to put Cardinal Manning's head into the picture for the same money – £1,000.' Millais's mischievous suggestion was not taken up. On 17 July Anne Pollen went to see the painting for herself: 'It is magnificent; it gives the dignity, gentleness and strength of his face; a most powerful portrait. Miss Millais said the Cardinal is a "beautiful old man" and seemed glad that we like the picture.'

At the end of 1881 Gladstone sent Newman evidence of seditious activity by priests in Ireland and asked him to make it known to the Pope. Newman's appreciation of the position of the Young Irelanders and his historical view made him careful in reply. He sought the advice of William Walsh, President of the Catholic University in Dublin, a nationalist and supporter of Sinn Fein, on what he saw as the probable justification of action by young Irish Patriots 'that the Irish people has never recognized, rather have and continuously since the time of Henry I I protested against and rejected the sovereignty of England, and have only seemingly admitted it only when they were too weak to resist; and therefore it is no sin to be what would be commonly called a rebel'. He later wrote to Gladstone, 'I think you overate [sic] the Pope's power in political and social matters. It is absolute in questions of theology, but not so in practical matters,' and told him that 'the intemperate, dangerous words of Priests and Curates' were for their respective bishops to deal with.

He was busy in other affairs as well. He did not let the inaccuracies of Tom Mozley's *Reminiscences chiefly of Oriel and the Oxford Movement* escape without censure: 'He finds a statement will not go on three legs, so from his imagination he adds a fourth.' The old master still took his students to task. And those who had learned from Newman continued to look up to him, even the sceptic, Mark Pattison on his death-bed, who wrote in reply to a compassionate note from Newman, 'When your letter, my dear master, was brought to my bedside this morning and I saw your well-known handwriting, my eyes filled so with tears that I could not at first see to read what you had said.'

Gladstone's Affirmation Bill caused trouble, and people sought Newman's views. Gladstone proposed that Charles Bradlaugh, elected for Northampton, an atheist, should be allowed to make an affirmation, instead of being sworn into Parliament. At once a rallying call was set up to all religious denominations in defence of the official recognition of God by the State. All the petitions were 'a piece of humbug' to Newman, and he had to make it publicly known that he saw no religious principle involved: the God sworn by in politics had little to do with the Personal God of the Jewish religion and Christianity. He wrote, 'Hence it little concerns religion whether Mr Bradlaugh swears by no God with the Government or swears by an Impersonal or Material, or abstract Ideal Something or other, which is all that is secured to us by the opposition.' The Bill though was rejected by the House of Commons.

Old age made him wary of accepting invitations. The Tennysons, through Aubrey de Vere, a past Professor of Political and Social Science at the Catholic University, asked him to stay at Aldworth, but he declined, writing to the poet that he accounted the invitation an honour as well as a kindness, 'I am of great age now – and though in good health, I am so full of the infirmities of old age, in so many respects, that I cannot leave home, unless I am compelled.' He did however visit the dying Mark Pattison at Oxford in January of 1884.

He continued writing. The following month in 1884 he published an article 'On the Inspiration of Scripture' in the *Nineteenth Century*; and later he was forced to come to his own defence after Lord Malmesbury had misrepresented him in his memoirs. In this year, too, he sat for a portrait by Emmeline Deane at the Oratory. She was to paint another, in oils, in 1888, which now hangs in the National Portrait Gallery.

Nor were these last years of Newman's life free from controversy. His views and integrity were attacked by the Congregationalist, A. M. Fairbairn, Principal of Airedale Theological College, Bradford, and soon to become first Principal of Mansfield College, Oxford. Fairbairn thought Newman distrusted Reason because his intellect was sceptical. Newman demonstrated his consistency of thought about Faith and Reason throughout the history of his writings and ended his last controversy with a finely judged riposte:

Marvellous is the power of a Fundamental View. There is said to have been a man who wrote English History, and could not be persuaded that the Heptarchy was over, or Queen Anne dead, I forget which; and who, when pressed with a succession of facts to the contrary, did but reply, as each came before him, 'O but, excuse me, *that* was an exception!' Dr Fairbairn reminds me of that man.

Although he remained mentally and intellectually active to the end of his life, from September 1886 when he was ill for a period, he became by stages physically weaker. His eyesight deteriorated, he kept falling, and his hands would not allow him to write without the greatest discomfort: increasingly he had to dictate his letters.

In August 1887 Ullathorne, whose retirement from his See had been announced, visited Newman. Such was Newman's humility that he kneeled for the bishop's blessing. Ullathorne, soon to be made a titular Archbishop, wrote, 'I felt annihilated in his presence, there is a saint in that man!'

In his penultimate year, he was still active, and naturally concerned enough to call on George Cadbury at the Bournville Works in Birmingham to discuss the compulsory attendance of Catholic girl employees at Cadbury's daily prayer meeting. Cadbury wrote to Edward Hymers, 'My brother and I saw him [Newman] and were charmed by the loving Christian spirit with which he entered into the question. He confirmed

50. A photograph of Newman taken in 1885 by Louis Barraud. He criticized it, the coat being worn, for 'advertising his poverty'

51. Cardinal Newman in May 1890, a few weeks before his death. 'Let us ever make it
our prayer and our endeavour, that we may know the whole counsel of God, and grow
into the measure of the stature of the fullness of Christ; that all prejudice and
self-confidence, and hollowness and unreality, and positiveness, and partisanship, may
be put away from us under the light of Wisdom, and the fire of Faith and Love; till we see
things as God sees them, with the judgement of His Spirit, and according to the mind of
Christ.'

your views and we promised him that we would, if possible, find some way
of meeting the difficulty without your flock suffering in any way.' In his
last year, Newman was able to give away the prizes at the School, and
attend the Latin play. It was in that summer, however, in his ninetieth
year, that he died.

Father William Neville who had looked after him in his last years, who
had been his constant companion, and acted as his amanuensis, described
his end. On the evening of 9 August Newman entered his room. Neville
had heard his footsteps, 'slow yet firm and elastic': his bearing was
'unbent, erect to the full height of his best days in the fifties; he was
without support of any kind. His whole carriage was, it may be said,
soldier-like, and so dignified; and his countenance was most attractive to
look at; even great age seemed to have gone from his face, and with it all
careworn signs; his very look conveyed the cheerfulness and gratitude of

his mind, and what he said was so kind; his voice was quite fresh and strong, his whole appearance was that of power, combined with complete calm.' It was as if he knew he was about to die.

That night he was taken ill with pneumonia. Although he got up the next morning, he had to return to bed immediately, and was later given the last Sacraments. He died at quarter to nine on the evening of 11 August, having been unconscious for most of that day.

Lord Rosebery visited the Oratory to see Newman lying in state, describing his corpse as a 'saint's remains over a high altar, waxy, distant, emaciated,' dressed in his Cardinal's habit. He commented, 'And this was the end of the young Calvinist, the Oxford don, the austere Vicar of St Mary's. It seemed as if a whole cycle of human thought and life were concentrated in that august repose. That was my overwhelming thought. Kindly light had led and guided Newman to this strange, brilliant, incomparable end.'

He was buried on 19 August at Rednal, according to his own instructions, in the grave of his old and beloved friend, Ambrose St John. Embroidered on his pall was his motto, '*Cor ad cor loquitur*', and on his memorial stone was his own chosen inscription, '*Ex umbris et imaginibus in veritatem*' – from shadows and images into truth.

52. Newman's grave at Rednal

Chapter 8   Literature and religion

'Saints are not literary men.'   J. H. Newman

John Henry Newman survives as one of the great and indisputable geniuses of the nineteenth century. As the years go by his reputation increases: his position in the history of English Literature, in the history of ideas, and in religion becomes more and more clear and well defined. In his own time, his writings made him known and respected. After the publication of the *Apologia*, there was no possibility of his being overlooked or forgotten. Yet even so, he had to combat within his own Church the extravagant notions of the ruling clique, the obstinate and arrogant 'faction', of Ultramontane bishops and superiors.

There was a quality about his writing which made him immediately intelligible both to clerics and laymen alike, a directness, simplicity and logic of expression, which gave his work impact and which made a deep impression on his readers. He is one of the greatest of English prose stylists in the nineteenth century, his *Apologia* and *Idea of a University* appearing in university literature syllabuses in the twentieth. It had long been supposed that the poetry of writers such as Newman and Keble would occupy that sort of place and have that considerable esteem. Their poetry, however, belongs to its own time and has little interest for the present, apart from some of the poems set to music as hymns and anthems.

Newman's prose style was the reward of a long apprenticeship.

Naturally, both at Dr Nicholas's School and at Oxford he studied the Classical authors, and we know from his own records that he copied styles of writers he admired: 'I seldom wrote without an eye to style and since my taste was bad, my style was bad. I wrote in style as another might write in verse, or sing instead of speaking, or dance instead of walking.' He read, too, the great English writers, the Anglican Divines of the seventeenth century, Andrewes, Laud, such men as Bishop Joseph Butler and Doctor Johnson. The product of this close observation of many ways of writing was a strong, plain, adaptable style which had emerged by the time he published *Tract 90* in 1841. It could accommodate many moods and tones, irony, scorn, humility, wonder, a colloquial directness, learned polemic, prayer and love.

Tract 90, entitled *Remarks on Certain Passages in the Thirty-nine Articles*, was an exercise in argument to show the compatibility of the Articles with Roman Catholicism. Newman had gone back to the study of history, a method of approach to argument and controversy that he was increasingly to use, and the tract's object was 'merely to show that, while our Prayer Book is acknowledged on all hands to be of Catholic origin, our Articles also, the offspring of an uncatholic age, are, through God's good providence, to say the least, not uncatholic, and may be subscribed by those who aim at being Catholic in heart and doctrine'. In the conclusion of the tract, Newman showed with serious irony that, while the Articles had been intended to exclude Catholic interpretation, at the same time that intention had failed. Since this was the case Catholics were not merely free, but rather obliged, to interpret them in a Catholic sense. Throughout, he argued closely from the text of the Articles, ingeniously examining the individual words and sentences, proving for example that Article XXI is right in declaring that General Councils may err, and have sometimes erred, unless it is promised by God that they shall not, as in the case of the Ecumenical Councils. Similarly, the Articles censured, not the authoritative and obligatory statements of the Roman Catholic Church, but merely the prevalent teaching of its officials. The tract also pointed out that since the Articles were drawn up before the Council of Trent was over, they could not have been directed against the decrees of that Council.

By resorting to history and arguing with great and deliberate care, Newman set out his case and proceeded to his conclusion. It was the pattern of what was to follow, whether he was arguing the development of Christian doctrine, or the development of his own religious opinions in the *Apologia*. Nor did his writing come easily: he took great pains over it. He wrote to his biographer, Wilfrid Ward, 'It is one of my sayings, (so continuously do I feel it) that the composition of a volume is like a gestation and child-birth.' To write was to fashion, to mould, to model like a true artist until perfection, or as near to it as possible, had been reached, no matter what the cost of energy and concentration. As he wrote:

My book on Justification ... I write, I write again: I write a third time in the course of six months. Then I take the third: I literally fill the paper with corrections, so that another person could not read it. I then write it out fair for the printer. I put it by; I take it up; I begin to correct again: it will not do. Alterations multiply, pages are rewritten, little lines sneak in and crawl about. The whole page is disfigured; I write again; I cannot count how many times this process is repeated.

This was his method, never easy, always arduous. Standing at his high desk for hours he worried away at the final form of his *Essay on the Development of Christian Doctrine*. His renunciation of the Church of England came before he had completed it, and was partly accomplished by his resorting to the principle of historical study. This method, too, had been proved and was to go on being so. Once again in clear, logical prose, composed with great dialectical skill, he anticipated, and accommodated, the theory of evolution in relation to the Church. He abandoned the old, received notion that Christianity originated as a complete dogmatic system issued by its first preachers. He admitted that the Church's creed had grown by a sure but gradual process, assimilating elements from all sides, and changing as the centuries passed. Newman's intellect proved that there was no inconsistency between the theory of evolution more than hinted at by Lyell, and finally expounded by Darwin. A theory which was shaking the faith of some, was accepted easily by Newman. He later confided to a friend that he was willing 'to go the whole hog with Darwin'.

His two best known prose works are *The Idea of a University; nine lectures addressed to the Catholics of Dublin* (1853), and the *Apologia pro Vita sua* (1864). Newman's own time at Oxford, both as student and teacher, had formed his ideas on what a university should be. His new university in Dublin should be an institution to make good Catholics ready for the world: it was not intended, as many of his episcopal superiors would have preferred, to exclude all that was thought dangerous in modern thought. He wrote in his controversial manner that a university:

... is not a convent; it is not a seminary; it is a place to fit men of the world for the world. We cannot possibly keep them from plunging into the world with all its ways and principles and maxims, when their time comes; but we can prepare them against what is inevitable; and it is not the way to learn to swim in troubled waters never to have gone into them. Proscribe, I do not merely say particular authors, particular passages, but Secular Literature as such; cut out from your class books all broad manifestations of the natural man; and these manifestations are waiting for your pupil's benefit at the very doors of your lecture-room in living and breathing substance ... you have refused him the masters of human thought, who would have in some sense educated him, because of their incidental corruption; you have shut up from him those whose thoughts strike home to our hearts; whose words are proverbs, whose names are indigenous to all the world, who are the standards of the mother tongue, and the pride and boast of their countrymen, Homer, Ariosto, Cervantes, Shakespeare, because the old Adam smelt rank in them; and for what have you reserved him? You have given him a liberty unto the multitudinous blasphemy of the day; you have made him free of its newspapers, its reviews, its magazines, its novels, its controversial pamphlets, of its Parliamentary debates, its law proceedings, its platform speeches, its songs, its drama, its theatre, of its enveloping, stifling atmosphere of death. You have succeeded but in this – in making the world his University.

Such was the wisdom of this Oratorian in process of setting up a new university. These discourses on the nature of a university are an example of Newman's Christian humanism. He warned against irreligious minds which prophesied the disproof of God and Revelation, and against religious minds which were 'jealous of the researches and prejudiced against the discoveries of science.' With commanding reassurance he addressed the faithful of the Church in forthright language of common sense. The Catholic, firmly believing in the Revelation of God, he declared:

... knows full well there is no science whatever but in the course of its extension runs the risk of infringing without any meaning of offence on its part the path of other sciences: and he knows also that if there be any one science which, from its sovereign and unassailable position, can calmly bear such unintentional colli-sions on the part of the children of earth, it is Theology. He is sure – and nothing shall make him doubt – that, if anything seems to be proved by astronomer, or geologist, or chronologist, or antiquarian, or ethnologist, in contradiction to the dogmas of faith, that point will eventually turn out, first, *not* to be proved, or secondly, not *contradictory*, or thirdly, not contradictory to anything *really revealed*, but to something which has been confused with revelation.

He made it clear, too, that free discussion was an absolute necessity: 'Now, while this free discussion is, to say the least, so safe for religion, or rather so expedient, it is on the other hand simply necessary for progress in Science.'

What is remarkable is that most of what Newman proposed and expounded was contrary to the views of the Catholic clerical establish-ment, but his ideas were promoted on behalf of the laity: as we have seen Newman was the champion of the laity, and nowhere more so than in his *Idea of a University*. He sought to persuade the Catholic hierarchy, and incidentally others of the Utilitarian school of thought, that knowledge was a good pursuit in its own right: 'Such is the constitution of the human mind, that any kind of knowledge, if it be really such, is its own reward.' He expanded on this theme:

The principle of real dignity in knowledge, its worth, its desirableness, considered irrespectively of its results, is this germ within it of a scientific or a philosophical process. This is how it comes to be an end in itself; this is why it admits of being called Liberal. Not to know the relative dispositions of things is the state of slaves or children; to have mapped out the Universe is the boast of Philosophy.

The purpose of a university education was plain, 'Liberal Education makes not the Christian, not the Catholic, but the gentleman. It is well to be a gentleman, it is well to have a cultivated intellect, a delicate taste, a candid, equitable, dispassionate mind; a noble and courteous bearing in the conduct of life – these are the con-natural qualities of a large knowl-edge; they are the objects of a University.' The aim was not to produce the man of fashion, someone who was at all times full of views. As he wrote in the preface to the discourses, 'It is almost thought a disgrace not to have a view at a moment's notice on any question from the Personal Advent to the Cholera or Mesmerism.' In the periodical literature of the day, there was never any shortage of information or theories. Anyone could gather a supply of details on any subject from religion to agriculture or the colonies. A university education, Newman warned, was not to be confused with picking up snatches of information here and there. On the contrary, it treated many subjects in depth, taught method, and encouraged fruitful study and enquiry. Newman's clear-headed thinking on the role and purpose of a university is still relevant and eminently readable.

The *Apologia* was, in a sense, an exercise in self-justification. He took the historical method, but applied it to his own life, the major part of the book being called *History of my Religious Opinions*. As well as answering Kingsley's charges in particular, the *Apologia* fulfilled a wider purpose: it made Newman's position in the Church of Rome clear to all his critics. That this purpose was intended is obvious in the way that Newman suppressed in the final publication, the more polemical and journalistic passages aimed at Kingsley personally.

As it survives in its final form, the *Apologia* is a masterpiece of moving prose, which embodies all of Newman's gifts, certainly his personality and powerful charm, and it transcends the reasons for its immediate composition. In it he refuted Kingsley's ill-founded accusations, and seized the opportunity to justify himself to all those who suspected his honesty of motive in embracing Roman Catholicism. He took on, as he said himself, not only his accuser but also those who considered themselves his judges.

Part V I I of the *Apologia* concerned the position of his mind since 1845: he considered that from the time he became Catholic, there was no further history of his religious opinions to relate. He wrote confidently:

I have been in perfect peace and contentment. I never have had one doubt. I was not conscious to myself, on my conversion, of any difference of thought or of temper from what I had before. I was not conscious of former faith in the fundamental truths of revelation, or of more self-command; I had not more fervour; but it was like coming into port after a rough sea; and my happiness on that score remains to this day without interruption.

The achievement of Part V I I of the *Apologia* was not attained without great sacrifice, and many pains. There was an urgency about answering Kingsley. His diary records that he sometimes spent sixteen hours a day in writing Part I I I, and on one occasion twenty-two hours of a day in writing Part V. He wrote to Hope-Scott in May of 1864, 'I never have been in such stress of brain and such pain of heart – and I have both trials together. Say some good prayers for me. I have been writing without interruption of Sundays since Easter Monday – five weeks – and I have at least three weeks more of the same work to come. I have been constantly in tears, and constantly crying out in distress. I am sure I never could say what I am saying in cold blood, or if I waited a month. . . .'

The *Apologia* made such a powerful impression on all parts of the thinking public that he was henceforth insured against eclipse which might have been brought about by the manoeuvrings of his ultramontane opponents. His position in the Church and his reputation in the world were secure. A later critic, both of literature and society, Lionel Trilling, has paid tribute to his genius, and the vital issues which he brings before the mind: '. . . the challenge that he offers to one's assumptions is so lively and so real, his sense of the world is so subtle and coherent, and his psychological perception is so complex and shrewd, that any reader who takes pleasure in endangering his own fixed ideas must be grateful for the exhilaration that Newman can give.'

After the *Apologia*, his most important literary work was *A Grammar of Assent* (1870). This, too, gave him great difficulty in its composition. He wrote to Aubrey de Vere in 1870, just after the essay had been published, that it was on a subject which had teased him for years, 'I felt I had something to say upon it, yet, whenever I attempted, the sight I saw vanished, plunged into a thicket, curled itself up like a hedgehog, or changed colours like a chameleon.' He made many beginnings over a series of years, but none would do. He went on, 'At last, four years ago, when I was up at Glion over the Lake of Geneva, a thought came into my head as the clue, the "Open Sesame", of the whole subject, and I at once wrote it down, and I pursued it about the Lake of Lucerne. Then when I came home I began in earnest, and have slowly got through it.'

He returned in this work to problems he had touched on before, of faith and reason, of the proper nature of belief. He held that belief or assent is a subjective act of apprehension, incapable of logical proof, though entirely rational. He argued that we reach certainties, not in the end through logic, but by intuitive perception, what he called the 'illative' sense, out of 'the cumulation of probabilities', and that these probabilities 'are too fine to avail separately, too subtle and circuitous to be convertible into syllogisms'. He argued that the 'living mind' of an individual determines the process of belief: 'It follows that what to one intellect is a proof is not so to another, and that the certainty of a proposition does properly consist in the certitude of the mind that contemplates it.'

The *Grammar* is a work of philosophy, psychology and literature. His arguments are illustrated by numerous examples, sometimes possessing a force of poetic beauty, sometimes upheld by a biting humour rarely seen in his other writings. It naturally attracted critics. A Jesuit scholar, Father Harper, criticized it. Newman's riposte was, 'Let those, who think I ought to be answered, those Catholics, first master the great difficulty, the great problem, and then, if they don't like my way of meeting it, find another. Syllogizing won't meet it.'

As well as being the author of tracts and treatises, he was also novelist and poet. He wrote two novels, *Loss and Gain* (1848) and *Callista* (1855). He gave *Callista* the subtitle of 'A Sketch of the Third Century'. The prefatory advertisements to successive editions show that the book was intended for Catholics: it depicted the Church as it was in the third century, and instructed Catholics how to behave in times of persecution. The heroine, Callista, is caught up in the clash between Christianity and pagan orthodoxy. The only possible, happy ending is her entry into Heaven. She is consequently martyred. Her sufferings, her torture, her death are described with unusual frankness and clarity for a novel of this period. It is a remorseless, and unforgettable novel.

Loss and Gain, subtitled 'The Story of A Convert', is fundamentally autobiographical, and therefore important as a fictional treatment of Newman's life. The novel is full of description of manners and society in the first half of the nineteenth century, and has many dramatic, humorous passages. Newman was prompted to write it, when he was sent a copy of a novel called *From Oxford to Rome* by a Companion Traveller in 1847. The author was in fact Elizabeth Harris. Newman found it 'wantonly and preposterously fanciful', and it provoked him to 'the production of a second tale; drawn up with a stricter regard to truth and probability ... showing as in a specimen, that those who were smitten with love of the Catholic Church, were nevertheless as able to write common-sense prose as other men'.

To an easily recognizable pattern, the novel traces the career of its young hero, Charles Reding, through the Anglican establishment of Oxford. About a third of the way through the novel, Charles finds himself in intellectual difficulties about the precise nature of the tenets of the Church of England. He is placed, prematurely for his year, in a lecture on the Thirty-nine Articles which he hopes will answer all the questions he has been asking about his religious beliefs. It did not live up to his hopes and a little later he remarks to a High Church bore called Bateman:

I hear so many different opinions in conversation; then I go to Church, and one preacher deals his blows at another; lastly, I betake myself to the Articles, and really I cannot make out what they would teach me. For instance, I cannot make out their doctrine about faith, about the sacraments, about predestination, about the Church, about the inspiration of Scripture.

Within the narrative this criticism represents an important step in the unsettling of Charles's religious convictions, and towards his eventual conversion to Roman Catholicism. Like Newman himself, at the end of the novel Charles is received into the Catholic Church by a Passionist priest.

Most of the novel is set in Oxford. There are glimpses of it at a distance as there are both in Hardy's *Jude the Obscure* and in Matthew Arnold's paean, *The Scholar Gypsy*, later on in the century. Returning to Oxford after two years absence, Charles views the panorama of the university, 'hallowed by many tender associations . . . There lay old Oxford before him, with its hills as gentle, and its meadows as green as ever. At the first view of that beloved place, he stood still with folded arms, unable to proceed.' There is a distinct ring of the romantic idyll about it. Yet there is also much ironic humour and near satire to underline what was wrong with the Oxford of his day, and the clerics who proceeded from it. Bateman had left Oxford and 'had accepted the incumbency of a church in a manufacturing town with a district of 10,000 souls, where he was full of plans for the introduction of the surplice and gilt candlestick among his people'. He pillories the Heads of the Colleges, supposedly religious men, but with immense incomes:

Here are the ministers of Christ with large incomes, living in finely furnished houses, with wives and families, and stately butlers and servants in livery, giving dinners all in the best style, condescending and gracious, waving their hands and mincing their words as if they were the cream of the earth, but without anything to make them clergymen but a black coat and a white tie. And then Bishops or Deans come, with women tucked under their arm; and they can't enter church but a fine powdered man runs first with a cushion for them to sit on, and a warm sheepskin to keep their feet from the stones.

The College tutor Vincent is shown as having a half-baked mind in spite of his reputation. He enjoyed good living rather than good learning: 'The young men even declared they could tell how much port he had taken in Common-room by the devoutness of his responsions in evening-chapel.' His breakfasts were second to none: 'The material part was easy enough; there were rolls, toast, muffins, eggs, cold lamb, strawberries on the table; and in due season the college-servant brought in mutton cutlets and broiled ham.' The difficulty came, Newman pointed out, when the accompaniment of thought, or at least words, was looked for, 'without which the breakfast would have been little better than a pig-trough'.

Sometimes Newman's humour is both ironical and direct, as when he sees entering a religious publisher's, a young Anglo-Catholic clergyman with a pretty girl on his arm, 'whom her dress pronounced to be a bride.

Love was in their eyes, joy in their voice, and affluence in their gait and bearing. Charles had a faintish feeling come over him: somewhat such as might beset a man on hearing a call for pork-chops when he was sea-sick.'

The *Athenaeum* condemned the novel for being 'flippant and farcical'. It possesses such elements, but there is seriousness, too, and a great deal of sympathy and affection, as well as censure, for both Oxford and the Church of England. Newman's great friend Keble is memorialized in the character of Charles Reding's vacation tutor, Carlton, 'so taking a man; so equable, so gentle, so considerate – he brings people together, and fills them with confidence in himself, and friendly feeling towards each other'. At times, his prose is poetic. The end of the summer vacation takes the student reading party indoors, away from their seated discussions upon the grass: 'Then came those fruits, the funeral feast of the year, mulberries and walnuts; the tasteless, juiceless walnut; the dark mulberry, juicy but severe, and mouldy withal, as gathered not from the tree, but from the damp earth. And thus the green spot weaned them from the love of it.'

There is much argument, and a great deal of introspection, in this autobiographical novel. There is a touch of farce towards the end, much as there is in Kingsley's contrasting novel *Yeast*. Yet there is a wealth of interest in it and, as *Fraser's Magazine* said, the story is told with 'skill and delicacy'.

In the same way that Newman made a contribution to the literature of the nineteenth century as a minor novelist, he did so too as a minor poet. He wrote more poems by far for the topical and partisan *Lyra Apostolica*, originally published in the *British Magazine*, than any of his friends. Of the 179 poems, he wrote 109: next was Keble with 46.

His two most famous poems are *The Pillar of the Cloud* and *The Dream of Gerontius*. The first was written when he was at sea in June 1833, voyaging from Sicily to Italy. It is a poem of utter conviction, confidence, and strong acceptance of God's steady guidance. The Poem's complete sincerity, and concentrated assurance are emphasized by the powerful double spondee in the second and fourth lines of each stanza:

Lead, Kindly Light, amid the encircling gloom,
　Lead Thou me on!
The night is dark, and I am far from home –
　Lead Thou me on!
Keep Thou my feet; I do not ask to see
The distant scene, – one step enough for me.

It is a tribute to Newman that this poem, above all the rest, survives popularly as an often-sung hymn set to J. B. Dykes's haunting tune 'Lux Benigna'.

The Dream of Gerontius attracted a greater composer, Elgar, and he set it to music as an oratorio. While driving himself almost to a pitch of nervous exhaustion in composing the *Apologia*, Newman experienced the feeling of approaching death. His imagination inspired, he composed the poem which traces the progress of Gerontius' soul from death-bed to Purgatory. Dying, he thinks he might sink:

> Into that shapeless, scopeless, blank abyss,
>   That utter nothingness, of which I came:

He calls on his friends to pray for him and, with the aid of the sacraments, passes from life to judgement in a state of grace. As a soul, he is escorted by an Angel, into the presence of the Divine Judge. Sustained by the Angel of the Agony, he is judged, and resigned he sings:

> Take me away,
> That sooner I may rise, and go above,
> And see Him in the truth of everlasting day.

The poem is moving and sincere. The narrative and commentary of the Guardian Angel is direct and clear. Above all, it has some beautiful, celebratory lyrics, which again survive as a well-known hymn:

> Praise to the Holiest in the height,
>   And in the depth be praise:
> In all His words most wonderful;
>   Most sure in all His ways!

Even so, only a small part of Newman's genius lies in his poetry. The greater part is in his prose. He admitted himself, 'I am hard-hearted towards the mere literary ethos, for there is nothing I despise and detest more.' He did not want to be a poet like Wordsworth or Tennyson, or a novelist like Scott, no matter how much he admired them. The real power of his intellect lay behind the style of his prose writings, in the controlled rhetoric of such a piece as this from his pamphlet, *The Tamworth Reading Room* (1841):

I consider, then, that intrinsically interesting and noble as are scientific pursuits, and worthy of a place in liberal education, and fruitful in temporal benefits to the community, still they are not, and cannot be, the *instrument* of an ethical training; that physics do not supply a basis, but only materials for religious sentiment; that knowledge does but occupy, does not form the mind; that apprehension of the unseen is the only known principle capable of subduing moral evil, educating the multitude, and organizing society; and that, whereas man is born for action, action flows not from inferences, but from impressions, – not from reasonings, but from Faith.

On a number of occasions, throughout his life, Newman felt that he had not long to live, and yet he knew at the same time that there was still much work, labours of Christian ministry in one form or another, left to do. It would seem that he was preserved to continue what he saw as his mission. In her diary for 18 July 1880, Anne Pollen recorded a story current at the Oratory, which she was told by Mr Pope, one of the masters of the school, when he was showing her around the church and school: Pope together with other Fathers and masters had witnessed the following, 'the Cardinal, while he was Doctor Newman, used to sit on the right side of the transept, in a special chair; one morning, he left church before the end of Mass, a thing he was hardly ever known to do. No sooner had he gone, than several bricks fell down from the wall behind, just on the place where his head would have been, had he stayed.' Newman's guardian angel looked after him on this specific occasion, as on others too: he clearly felt that he had been allowed to emerge from the valley of the shadow of death after his typhoid illness in Sicily.

He lived for almost a further sixty years. The sum of his work was, in the end, prodigious. Apart from anything else he did, he wrote a mass of treatises, tracts, poems, sermons, lectures and letters. These alone stand as a monument to his tireless genius. Yet in brick and stone, his real monument stands as the Birmingham Oratory itself.

He knew only too well that one day he would suffer the attentions of successive biographers, and he had strict ideas on how they should perform their task. In a letter to Jemima he delivered his considered opinion:

A much higher desideratum than interest in Biography is met by the method, (as it may be called,) of Correspondence. Biographers varnish; they assign motives; they conjecture feelings; they interpret Lord Burleigh's nods; they palliate or defend. For myself, I sincerely wish to seem neither better nor worse than I am. I detest suppression; and here is the great difficulty. It may be said to ask a biographer to edit letters is like putting salt on a bird's tail. How can you secure his fidelity? He must take care not to hurt people, make mischief, or get into controversy. Hence men like Talleyrand, have forbade the publication of their correspondence till a thirty years have passed since their death, that the existing generation may have fairly died out. But party interests and party feelings never die out; and how can one promise oneself that men thirty years hence, whom one has never seen, into whose hands one's MSS come, will be above the influence of party motives, at a time when personal delicacies and difficulties are in their graves? It is very seldom that correspondence can be given *in extenso* by reason of its prolixity. There must necessarily be a selection of passages; sometimes one half sentence alone is valuable in a whole letter, and that, very valuable: but it may tell on this side a controversy, or on that: and whether it sees the light or not will depend upon the perspicacity or straight-forwardness of an Editor.

The editors of Newman's letters and diaries have tried to ensure, according to his wishes, that his correspondence does speak for him. Biographers of Newman must do the best they can by his instructions and their own lights. Imaginative content, 'the interpretation of Lord Burleigh's nods', ought to be avoided.

The final assessment of Newman, however, must be as the biographer sees it according to the evidence that he has discovered. There can be little doubt that as a young man he was ambitious with more than a hint about him of intellectual arrogance. He was expected to do well in the Oxford Final Degree examinations, but a streak of asceticism made him too weak for the ordeal. Copeland confided to Alfred Plummer, a Fellow of Trinity, that Newman had the Neo-Platonic idea that the more he reduced his body, the better his mind would work, and that he almost starved himself before going into the Schools, 'The whole time of the examination he was physically unfit for any such strain. The wonder is that he got any class at all.' He was, as we know, placed in the second division of the Second Class with ten others. Below them there was a Third Class of seventy-four. To contemplate entering competition for an Oriel Fellowship after that result required great self-confidence and assurance. Oriel was intellectually the leading College in Oxford: its Fellowship glittered with stars as no other college at that time did. It is recorded in a Trinity College Breviarium of stories about Thomas Short, Newman's tutor there, that Short related: 'You know it was an object of great importance to Newman at that time to obtain a Fellowship. For his father, who was a brewer at Alton, had just failed. I had occasion to call on Copleston the Provost, while the Fellowship examination was going on, and I took the opportunity of saying to him, "Mr Newman of my College is a very deserving man, and the circumstances of his family at the present time are such as to make a Fellowship a great object to him." Copleston said, "I thank you for the information; for such considerations are not altogether without weight in our elections!"' Whatever the considerations were in the end, at the time of the examination Newman felt he had broken down. 'I have made a complete mess of it,' he told Short; but Short met Tyler, a Fellow of Oriel, by chance, who said, 'Tell me something about your man Newman, for he has written by far the best essay.' This information enabled Short to encourage Newman, who was misjudging his own performance, to continue, to work through 'as if you had no chance and were only an unconcerned spectator.' Newman was duly elected and became one of that most distinguished set of Oxford intellectuals. After such false starts and break-downs, in his Degree and Fellowship examinations, what a sense of final achievement, and security, Newman must have obtained by his establishment in the Oriel Common Room.

His diaries and journals tell of his struggle against self-will when he was on his Sicilian journey, and of the dangers of self-delusion when he thought he might accompany Whately to Dublin. Self-will and intellectual arrogance might well have spurred him on in his opposition to Dr Hampden which lasted some years. If Hampden was victim of an organized campaign against him, then Newman carries greatest responsibility for its leadership. It is a fact that Hampden was elected Professor of Moral Philosophy in 1834 when Newman considered himself a most proper and better candidate for the chair. Newman was undeniably disappointed by his failure to secure it.

Yet these are evidences of the failings of a young man, self-assured, confirmed in the esteem of his own abilities by the prizes already won, alert and energetic. As he matured, and as his religious faith itself matured with his constant recourse to, and study of, history, so his nature became more settled and in a real sense more disciplined. When he changed his spiritual allegiance to the See of Rome, he took with him a strength of character which had developed throughout his Oxford, Anglican years. In future struggles, with the Catholic hierarchy, with Oratorians, or with personal adversaries such as Kingsley, he brought to bear on his opponents a firmness of mind and a fairness of judgement which his preceding experience had given him.

Inevitably the Roman Catholic Church has reaped the benefits of Newman's great pastoral ministry and of his scholarship. From the first days of his Oriel Fellowship he filled with exceptional ability the rôles of preacher, confessor, teacher, confidant and counsellor. He soon saw that his parish extended farther than the bounds of Oxford, then farther than the bounds of Birmingham, and became in effect the whole of intellectual England.

As an Anglican he helped make the Church of England conscious of its historical roots and of its essential catholicity. As a Roman Catholic, part of his major work was to oppose the extravagances of other converts who had succeeded to power in the hierarchy, such as Faber and Ward. Their attempts to introduce continental forms of worship into England he resisted with all the power of his influence and rhetoric. Their extreme, ultramontane interpretation of Papal Infallibility, he also argued strenuously against. He was always the most English of Catholics, and attracted the support of many old Catholic families. He championed the laity at a time when it was not acceptable to do so. He pursued what he saw as right, what he saw as the truth, even when it incurred the disfavour of the powerful in Rome. When the first Vatican Council came to an end, and a definition of Papal Infallibility had been made, it seemed that Newman's ideas were in eclipse. Yet his ideas, in appropriate keeping with his own theories, took root and developed, flowering in the work of the second Vatican Council some hundred years later. Bishop B. C. Butler gave as his verdict of the later Council:

The tide has been turned and a first, immensely important, step has been taken towards vindication of all the main theological, religious and cultural positions of the former Fellow of Oriel.

It finally showed that the Catholic Church had at last accepted the principles of historical development. Again, as Bishop Butler wrote, the Church was able 'to turn her eyes and desires outwards from a somewhat unhealthy introspection to the challenges and needs of a world tremendously alive and in a phase of incalculably swift evolution'. He has described Newman as possessing in retrospect 'a sort of prophetic charisma, as one who, because he knew of only two absolutely luminous realities, God and his own soul, was able not only to diagnose the evils of his own day but to see beyond them to the abiding purposes of the God of our salvation'.

The second Vatican Council also made it possible for the Roman Catholic Church to invite other Christians to join in dialogue about differences and so gradually to bring about an approach towards unity within the Christian Church. In a way Newman was the symbol of such a proposition. He knew dearly two Churches, and in his time was a leader of both. Opposed to extremes, he served, and his ideas still serve, as a bridge towards the understanding of them both.

It should not be forgotten that there were other continental Roman Catholics who expounded similar ideas to Newman's, Dupanloup in France, and Döllinger in Germany. Plummer, the Fellow of Trinity, recorded how he acted as an intermediary between Newman and Döllinger, 'They did not quite like to correspond directly but each said or wrote to me what he was pretty sure that I should pass on to the other.' Newman, however, was the most forward-looking. He wanted Catholics to accept responsibilities in the world, exert their influence for the good, assert themselves, broaden their minds knowing all the time where truth lay; and he wanted them to be guided like fully responsible people by their educated and enlightened consciences.

The old Cardinal had been the moving spirit in a great revolution of thought. He was a prolific writer, and editor of journals, the founder of both a school and a university, and the first Superior of the Oratory in England. His work had an inestimable influence on the religious life not only of England, but of every country associated with the Roman communion, and that influence still lives on.

Characteristic of Newman was his reaction to news that a friend considered him to be a saint. The sense of his own inadequacies was very strong: his reproof to his friend given by way of a third party correspondent was gentle and amusing, and serves as a final, fitting reminder of his humility and his own mature assessment of himself.

I have nothing of a saint about me as everyone knows, and it is a severe (and salutary) mortification to be thought next door to one. I may have a high view of many things, but it is the consequence of education and a peculiar cast of intellect – but this is very different from *being* what I admire. I have no tendency to be a saint – it is a sad thing to say so. Saints are not literary men, they do not love the classics, they do not write Tales. I may be well enough in my way, but it is not the 'high line'. People ought to feel this, most people do. But those who are at a distance have exalted notions about one. It is enough for me to black the saints' shoes – if St. Philip uses blacking in heaven.

53. A bust of John Henry, Cardinal Newman by A. Broadbent against the Garden Quad of Trinity College, Oxford. 'Trinity had never been unkind to me. There used to be much snap-dragon growing on the walls opposite my freshman's rooms there, and I had for years taken it as an emblem of my own perpetual residence even unto death in my University.'

Index